DON'T SHOOT
THE MULES!

DON'T SHOOT THE MULES!

JIM HOUGH

1939-40 323211 Trooper Cheshire Yeomanry
1940 323211 Gunner and Bombardier Royal Artillery
1943 190147 Captain Queen's Royal Regiment
and Animal Officer 14th Army
1944 190147 Co-editor Official Troops Newspaper BAOR
(British Army of the Rhine)

authorHOUSE®

AuthorHouse™
1663 Liberty Drive
Bloomington, IN 47403
www.authorhouse.com
Phone: 1-800-839-8640

First published by AuthorHouse   09/17/2011

ISBN: 978-1-4670-0033-8 (sc)
ISBN: 978-1-4670-0034-5 (ebk)

Printed in the United States of America

For Tessa...

CONTENTS

Wartime reminiscences of:

This is one of many tens of thousands of Japanese Government Treasury notes ransacked by British Chindit troops after an ambush on a Japanese Army motorised convoy on the Burma Road near Imphal in November 1943.

FRONT   REVERSE
Actual Size 5.5× 3.5ins.

One of the trucks in the convoy, which was escorted by motor cycle outriders, was carrying huge amounts of cash with which to pay their front line troops and for supplies from Burmese collaborators.

Armed guards were seen leaping from the truck and although raked with fire from sten guns and carbines by the Chindits, many escaped unhurt into the adjoining jungle. Some joined the lines of Japanese deserters already on the long trudge back to Rangoon.

The Chindits were quick to realise the enormity of their haul. Some of them, having filled their pockets with banknotes, stuffed further wads down their trousers gaiters and shirt fronts. Haversacks were emptied of spare clothing, socks, ground sheets and other essentials. All were discarded to make more room for money. Disposal of government property in this fashion is an offence under military discipline. It was widely ignored. There was much talk of buying hotels in Bombay to finance lifetimes of wanton women and slothful splendour after the war.

The above illustration is a scanned copy and does not reveal the meticulous workmanship of the Japanese engraver. Closer examination also showed that the notes had no serial number. This small point sowed seeds of suspicion. It was not long before the dreadful truth was exposed. The notes were worthless. Not forgeries but unbacked by any recognised banking system and therefore not negotiable.

I tried to appease the men by saying that they should hold on to some notes because one day they might have some small value as souvenirs or curiosities.

The advice was ignored.

*   *   *

On September 4, 1939 War broke out. I was mobilised into the Cheshire Yeomanry, also known as the Prince of Wales's Bodyguard, a Territorial regiment and provided with an old racehorse called Red King, a sword, a scabbard put it in and a Lee Enfield.303 rifle with leather rifle bucket left over from the Great War. Thus equipped I was considered adequately armed to launch attacks on panzer tanks alongside our brave allies in Poland. A few days later Red King, whose Cheshire owner had been persuaded to sell him to the Army for £20, in effect a shameless confiscation, but there was a war on and I were charging across Salisbury Plain, sixteen abreast, with drawn swords, at the full gallop, at an equine pace known by my new colleagues as "split-arse". Had Red King put a foot in a rabbit hole he might have broken a leg. I might have broken my neck. It was supposed to make men of us.

Mercifully this nonsense was suspended after a few days when Winston Churchill, prodded by the Daily Mirror and every mum in the land with a boy of 18, decreed that no boy under 19 should be sent on combative duties abroad. Our Regiment was under notice to be transferred almost immediately to Palestine where, as usual, they had their own war going on. My part in the enterprise and that of all other Cheshire yeomen was cancelled and half a trainload of we underage remnants was dispatched to Lincoln to join the newly-formed 39th Light Anti-Aircraft battery, Royal Artillery. We were proud of being His Majesty's yeomen, and stood before our new commanding officer wearing our smartly-cut breeches with strapping in becoming shades of rust or lemon (both illegal except to officers) and a khaki tunic, also a hangover from the Great War, but ripped apart, re-cut and re-made by a tailor in Chester to a more acceptable style at our own expense. Over this was a leather bandolier, polished with just the right mixture of dark tan boot polish and spit to produce a finish one could see one's face in. We were informed by the C.O., whose name I have forgotten, and have no wish to recall, that we resembled a bunch of dissolute Mexican desperado bandits. Forthwith we must visit the quartermaster's stores and exchange our absurd garb for regulation battledress, steel helmets and ammunition boots. With that we were formed into three ranks and marched through the streets of Lincoln to our quarters for the night which was an old drill hall with no heating, chairs or table. In the middle of the floor was a large stack of straw, none too clean and a pile of paliasses (canvas mattress covers.) We stuffed them full with the straw and ill grace and had a sleepless night.

It should be explained why, when with the Yeomanry, all of us went to so much trouble and expense to look smart with fancy strapping etc. beyond the bounds of necessity. Every night a number of us were detailed for guard duty.

This was a hated and largely useless chore which deprived us of much-needed rest and sleep. Days in the Yeomanry were long and hard. Those selected for this duty reported to the Guard Room, which usually doubled as the Orderly room or general office. They lined up for inspection by the orderly officer who scrutinised all in the closest detail. Rifles, personal cleanliness and hair length (short back and sides) were given particular attention. All had to be absolutely clean, correct and acceptable. So that rifle barrels could be properly examined the rifle bolt was drawn back and the soldier placed his thumb over the barrel entrance. The thumb nail, if it had been scrubbed, reflected some light when the officer looked down the barrel. Whether clean or not the officer said nothing and moved on to repeat the performance on the next man. When all had been inspected the men were drawn up to attention by the Sergeant in charge for an important procedure known as The Stick. While all breaths were bated, the officer moved slowly round the ranks, giving a long, lingering stare at each man. Then, after a prolonged think, tapped two of them on a shoulder with his leather-covered swagger stick. They each took a step forward, gave a smart salute and marched off to the pub or the pictures. No Guard duty for them. It pays to look smart in the Army.

On the way to breakfast next day we were apprehended by the Colonel who enquired why we were still improperly dressed as banditos. We replied that the quartermaster did not have any battledresses of our size but, we were assured, we told him, that they were on order and would be with us in a day or two and we were so much looking forward to having them.

Suddenly, overnight and without warning and, in typical army style, no apparent reason, we were uplifted from our loathsome Lincoln billet to new headquarters at Scunthorpe, Normanby Hall. The Yeomanry boys had not proved good at assimilation with the rest of the regiment and the independent coterie which we now formed was known as The Boudoir Boys because we wore pyjamas in paliasses, used scented shaving cream and conversed in supposedly affected accents. The Boudoir Boys, because of their superior cunning, intuition and common sense, soon sorted out the best jobs for themselves at Normanby and I was doubly promoted from the rank of Gunner to Bombadier because I could read and write. Standards of literacy and numeracy in the Army were appallingly low. Had it been known, it was said, that I could also do long division I would have been put up for a commission. That would be more than a year ahead as wheels of progress in the Army ground exceeding slow.

I was glad to leave Lincoln, hopefully for ever. It was a dull town. No pubs worth talking about, no theatre, no cinema, no skating rink, no dance hall. There was a cathedral. Fine for those into cathedrals. We were not.

The most pleasing aspect of my promotion was that my pay shot up from two shillings a day to 35/-a-week. Two shillings a day, one might suppose, would be fourteen shillings a week. Not in the Cheshire Yeomanry. I received only ten shillings a week because four shillings was detained by the quartermaster for "barrack damages". A further nine pence a week was retained for National Insurance stamps which did not apply to the Army. Since the PeninsularWar all army quartermasters had been on the fiddle. When I protested that there had been no barrack damage in my time this was agreed but, it was explained, a contingency fund was required in case some occurred in future. With our change of address and a new commanding officer with more pressing matters requiring his attention, the campaign to attire us in battledress and steel helmets fizzled out. We were now even more determined to retain our Yeomanry attire as it was scoring quite a hit with the Scunthorpe girls. They wanted to know what we kept in those funny little pouches. As though we would tell them. One of our number, Peter Ridout, a good looking boy with a moustache, who was 19 but looked 30, a front row prop in his home rugby team, and much later Town Clerk of Amersham, had picked up a lovely girl called Cherry at a bus stop. He offered to introduce me. Cherry said she had a sister at home called Pauline whom she knew I would like. The Three of us linked arms and marched off in the snow (because it was snowing) to her house in Vicarage Road where I was presented to Pauline and her mother, who asked me to call her Cristobel. There was a father there. It was immediately apparent that Cristobel was infinitely more attractive than Pauline. Apparently she was an expert with the Daily Telegraph cryptic crossword puzzle which had just been invented. She could skip through it in ten minutes. To do this, she said, one had to get inside the compiler's mind. She explained how this was done and may she have a go at getting inside my mind? Of course, I said yes and she puffed up the cushions and moved in a bit closer.

My new and larger disposable income was burning a hole in my pocket and it was necessary to dispose of some of it before it exploded in flames. Top of the list of urgent requirements was a new pair of shoes. My heavy black ammunition boots, with vicious solid steel studs, toe-caps and half-heels were damaging my feet. They would also have damaged Pauline's had I persisted in wearing them for the Palais Glide.

Hitherto my mother had always selected and paid for my shoes. I was not totally confident about undertaking this task myself. I solicited the aid of Pauline who kindly offered to help. We agreed to meet outside Stead and Simpson in Scunthorpe High Street next day.

It was easy for me to arrange a day off for this as alongside my promotion had come a new post involving charge of thirty men. This mantle of responsibility fell upon my shoulders easily and naturally. I did not have to ask anybody for time off to go shopping. I just put my hat and coat on and went, barking out a few orders as I closed the door.

At the shoe shop the first "S" of the fascia had fallen of had fallen off, leaving only "TEAD AND SIMPSON". It will be recalled that the Prince of Wales (later King in waiting as Edward VIII), was widely known as Ted and he had been involved in an extra-marital dalliance with an American divorcée, Wallis Simpson. Both of them should have known better. The manager told me it worked wonders for business.

I had seen in the window a pair of brown brogues which took my fancy at 25/-. Pauline sensibly dismissed these as the price took too much of my budget and all those small holes, she said, would eventually let the rain in. We set about examining the shop's entire stock of men's shoes and when the floor was piled high with empty white boxes Pauline said we really must try Truefit before making a decision. I offered to help rebox everything but Ted and Simpson would not hear of it. Clothes rationing, imposed by coupons, was already in force but did not yet apply to shoes. This was late 1939 and all the shops were mostly still well stocked with consumer goods They began to empty quickly early in 1940.

Truefit had some similar brown brogues at 19/—which I hastily acquired before somebody else. They were very good quality and lasted for years before collapsing in India. An itinerant cobbler, squatting by the roadside, quickly made bespoke replacements. First, measurements were required. He placed my foot on a sheet of white paper and drew a pencilled line round it. He barely bothered to look at it because, in the very hot weather my sweaty sock had already left a clear outline and a perfect pattern. Instep measurements were taken with a tape measure. The shoes were ready when I called the next day. They were excellent, just as good as my Truefit beauties and also served me well for years.

I was now rich. Or comparatively. My bombardier's pay, much more than I had at any other time in my life, except in brief periods after Christmas before the pound notes and even fivers given by kind and generous aunts and uncles had evaporated.

Lincoln and Scunthorpe are in the same county, thirty miles equidistant. The inhabitants could be in different planets. Scunthorpe folk are kind, generous, patient, intelligent and considerate. They are industrious, good at hot mill steel rolling and willing to start again at a moment's notice. Their particular virtue, instilled at birth and nurtured until old enough to drink alcohol, is a natural tendency to be welcoming, helpful, kind and hospitable to strangers. A traveller on the road, tired, hungry, thirsty and perhaps weary and disoriented, might, in his exhaustion, might find himself flopping though the open door of The Owl, a noted hostelry in High Street, whose door has never been known to be closed even after statutory hours of business. Our new friend, (all strangers are immediately friends in Scunthorpe), is offered a drink. A refusal might incur offence or hurt feelings. If such a refusal were explained or excused on grounds of just having had one it would be taken as rude, churlish and unreasonable. Two immensely strong arms would be then tightly clasped round a protester's waist, the body raised from the ground and rotated through 180 degrees. Restored to upright, a pint of Tolly's is sluiced down the throat while the mouth is open, yelling for help. It was a pleasure to be with such an entertaining and friendly crowd.

A favoured place of entertainment in Scunthorpe in 1939/40 was not the pub but a variety theatre, the Savoy. Best seats were three shillings and sixpence. Servicemen in uniform could sit anywhere for a shilling (5p). I always sat in the front row and kept an eye on the band. There was a pretty and very talented lady pianist who was second in my imagined affections only to Cristobel. There was a violin, a tenor sax, a trumpet and a drum kit. The artistes were from the huge number who travelled round the country making a precarious living "doing the halls." Among them was Tom Mix. This was not bingo speak for six but an American singing cowboy with a white horse who did stunts with a lariat and sang mournful songs about being all alone on the prairie and who could be surprised. Poor Tom was trapped here by the war. He went back alone to the States and his horse went to the Leicestershire Yeomanry. Among the band of artistes playing the country, were several soubrettes. Soubrettes, like Pierrots, have long ago disappeared. They were multi-talented young females who could recite funny poems in regional accents, sing, tap dance and yodel to a percussion accompaniment by tambourine, an instrument which was activated, one can hardly say played, by being slapped on thighs and, daringly, on bottoms with saucy smiles and winks to boys in the audience. A notable exponent was Betty Driver, then 16, who survived this perilous existence to be become, fifty years later, a stalwart resident of Coronation Street, a soap. She used to enter the stage with flying cartwheels and perform elementary acrobatic routines culminating, on gala nights, to rapturous and thunderous applause, the splits.

There was an alternative theatre in Scunthorpe, at The Owl which had a well equipped stage with footlights, overhead floods and spots. The entertainment was a non-stop discovery talent show. Standing up at the back, at the bar and noisily showing off with the lads, was free. Metropolitan sophistication was provided by curtains which whizzed to and fro as required at a touch of a button and with great speed if required which would be if enthusiasm for any turn started to wane.

I am not abnormally fickle by nature but in passage of time I went off Betty Driver and, to be totally truthful, and also and possibly rather meanly, Cristobel.

A new love in, my life, regrettably totally unrequited, was Dinah Sheridan, a startlingly beautiful West End actress who had had left London to escape the bombs and earn a living in the provinces. Since the start of the War theatre opportunities outside London were few. She found a billet with a small repertory company in Llandridrod Wells. There were other distinguished thespians there including Sybil Thorndike and her husband, Lewis Casson. The theatre, grandly called The Albert Hall, was very small, about 100 seats and then only if crammed in uncomfortably very close together. I had left Scunthorpe and was in this delightful Welsh spa town for three months in 1941, on an intensive course learning to be an artillery gunnery officer and living in the 5-star Metropole hotel, quite a change from a Nissen hut on a slag bank in

Scunthorpe. The course was incredibly hard and tiring work with little opportunity for recreation. My one big treat was a weekly visit to The Albert Hall, a tiny theatre squashed into a row of shops and once a Baptist chapel. I saw some amazingly talented productions there, often drawing room dramas by J.B. Priestley. There was massive competition for tickets but there were always ways and means. Do not try to find the Albert Hall now because it has been chopped down. It is on the outskirts, housed in what looks like a large, rotting battery chicken complex. It's only hope is for a Baptist revival. Shops have reappeared where the old ones used to be.

In about 1975 Dinah walked into a shop of mine in Kensington Church Street, London, so I reintroduced myself. She looked at me politely but blankly and I explained I had seen her several times at the Albert Hall. She then looked at her companion, a lady. Have I ever played the Albert Hall? Dinah enquired. Don't think so, darling, was the reply. I don't mean the London Albert Hall, I said. I mean the proper one. The real one. The one in Llandrindrod Wells. It was nice to see her laughing.

Another thought about the theatre at the Owl which puzzled me at the time and has done for years. When the curtains were redrawn it was by an electric motor which automatically cut off when they were in the closed position. That, one thought, would be that. Finito. But no. For a time, maybe ten or twenty seconds, the curtains would slowly but surely shimmy up and down, rhythmically, like a Colombian who is incapable of standing still if some rap music is playing anywhere within miles. Thumbs and forefingers snap and the body responds to an unheard beat and rhythm. The Owl curtains behaved in the same way. I cannot believe that some unknown divine or surreal power was responsible. Not in The Owl. The worrying conclusion is that in any case it does not matter and if I continue to worry about it only confirms my belief that total pottiness fast approaches.

**The Boudoir Boys at Cark-inCartmel Firing Camp (see p3)
June 1940
Ken Taylor, Peter Ridout, Neil Heap, Jim Hough,
Leslie Stone, Arthur Cooper, Peter Rowlands**

In June 1940 there was a prolonged heat wave. The B.E.F. had been a total failure and was evacuating France via Dunkirk. There was a threat of invasion by German forces. At long last our useless gunnery was replaced by modern 40mm Bofors automatic canons, superbly efficient weapons, developed and marketed by the Czechs and sold by them to both England and Germany at first but later exclusively to Britain.

I and my company went on a firing course at Cark-in-Cartmel, near Morecambe Bay, to learn how to use them. We fired live explosive shells at a sleeve towed by a biplane at about 50m.ph over the sea. Highly dangerous for its pilot but all survived.

It was now nearing time for our first action. Until now we had been playing at soldiers. German hedge-hopping low-level fighter-bombers had been straffing the RAF airfield at North Coates, near Grimsby. Our Beau fighters and ground defences were also targets of the Germans who were a constant threat with their daylight and night-time raids, both now occurring almost daily. The raiders needed to be put out of action. In addition, there was now considered to be an even more dangerous threat from the sea—an invasion. The South coast was ruled out because if Hitler intended to invade across the Channel he would have done so by now. The East Anglian coast was a more likely option. It was therefore decided to kill two Goliaths with a single slingshot, as it were, by sending our five bofors guns to North Coates where they could discourage German straffers and air raiders and maybe even shoot one down, you never know your luck in a war. The guns could be sited where they could double as field artillery on the coastline. Six bofors shells into even the biggest assault landing craft would blow it out of the water.

With no red tape or movement order we set off at once, five guns and five quads to tow them and each seating gun crews of five plus me. Quads were large, ungainly vehicles, quadrangle in shape, hence the name, allegedly armour—plated but that was a downright lie, mechanically unreliable and made by the British Bedford Motor Co. who should have been ashamed of themselves especially as I had written to their MD tell him so. I much preferred Jeeps. Tougher. More manoeuvrable and could winch themselves out of any trouble. This was the last occasion on which I personally used quads although use of Jeeps as gun tractors was forbidden in the Army on the grounds that this use might ruin the clutch plates. I continued to do so, thereby risking, believe it or not, a court martial. My defence would have been that I knew a lieutenant in the US army who would do anything for a British buddy and had 1,600 spare Jeep clutch plates in stock, do'in nothin' and would supply and fit any time no charge no problem. He could also supply me with his .22 automatic carbine repeater rifle, guaranteed as used by the Chicago Mafia, for the bargain price of twenty chips (rupees or 30 shillings.) I told the sergeant that losing or selling one's weapon in the British Army was a desperately serious offence, considered treason. He seemed unperturbed. All he had to do was tell the quartermaster he had lost it and he would be given another. I had a free trial and could see that it was hugely superior to any similar weapon our army had and would have been invaluable in Burma. (Like a complete fool I turned it in at the first arms amnesty after the War).

On arrival at the airfield the battery C.O. was there to direct us to our sites. The first was just twenty yards up the perimeter road, grassy plot, fairly level uninterrupted visibility and ideal for our purpose. The crew detached the gun and pulled it into the position I had indicated, awaiting my order ACTION STATIONS! before swinging into the drill we had all practised a hundred, perhaps a thousand times before. Two men would swing the lateral arm out then furiously turn the crank handles which lowered the feet, the front and rear arms, then load the magazine with a clip of five high explosive shells. The record to that point was thirteen seconds . . . the heavens above suddenly erupted and spilt open with a deafening cacophony of sound and ear-splitting roar which numbed the senses. I glanced up. There was a man there. He was in an aeroplane, wearing a cap, in the nose cone. Not twenty yards away. He was firing a twin-barrelled gun. Straight at me. He looked not unlike me. High explosive shells raked the ground around me. This was it. I will be dead. I was totally paralysed with shock. Not fright. Shock. Shock is different. Not a muscle in my body moved. If you have never experienced this sensation I can tell you how it feels. You feel empty. Totally empty. Nothing inside you. No flesh, no bones. No blood. No feeling. Only bells. Why bells? I very distinctly heard bells. The plane zoomed up into the sky, five hundred feet in as many seconds as it banked and swooped down again at full throttle, all guns blazing, to try to kill us all again. We were no longer frozen with shock. We were in that ditch, at the side of the road. Pressing our bodies into the damp earth as far as they would go . . . then—*BANG!* Down we went into the ditch again. The next gun site up the road had partly recovered from their shock paralysis and in panic, possibly horrified at having done nothing, had slammed a shell into the breech and pulled the trigger. A futile gesture and a waste of ammunition for which they were severely bollocked by me later.

North Coates went quiet. Hedge-hopping raids ceased. Although terrifying, very little damage was caused and it was decided to return the guns to Scunthorpe where they were perhaps more needed. On arrival back at my hut there was a note on the bed, from the C.O., saying I had been recommended for a commission. I was to report to a Selection Board at an address is Spalding, Lincs. at 9am the next day and had to catch the 6am milk train from Scunthorpe to Grimsby *at 5.30*a.m. Then change to the Spalding train at *7.05*am. Having trudged home through the deep snow after my soldier's farewell to Pauline I was in no fit state to go anywhere. My greatcoat buttons needed polishing, so did my boots. I needed a shower and a shave. There was not time for all this, so I awoke Gunner Dancer and requested him, very politely, just to please me, to awake, get up and clean my buttons and boots. The answer I received was too too offensive reproduce here. I offered to give him 10 shillings. The reposte was even more vulgar. But when I upped the stake to £2, he shot out of bed at once and set to work with a will. I was soon trudging off to Scunthorpe again, to the station. It was still snowing heavily and I was spoiling my beautifully polished boots. That could not be helped. On the train, I had time to gather my thoughts. These were that it was vitally important that I pass the selection board's interview. (Approval of this did not mean an automatic commission, just a recommendation that I be considered for an OCTU course). It was important because so far in life I had achieved virtually nothing, my two stripes as a Bombadier were of insignificant importance. A commission would surely give me a leg up when I went back to civilian life after the war. I no longer had the slightest intention of resuming my career as an estate agent's clerk. Also, more money would mean a more comfortable life in the army, but I had to look the part first and I had not yet had a shave. On arrival at Spalding I walked down the main street and to my surprise and delight saw a Salvation Army canteen, a blaze of light and up and running even at that early hour. I went in and had a good breakfast. After that I looked for a barber. There was one nearby but he had not yet opened for business. With an impertinence which I recognised at the time but felt I could ignore, I threw up a handful of pebbles at a bedroom window. The window flew up and a male face appeared. I told the man that, as a matter of life and death, I had to have a shave and hair cut immediately. If only he would come downstairs I would explain the reason to him and also give him £3. To the man's credit, he came down and opened the door, heard my story and told me to sit down in the barber's chair. After my shave and shampoo I gave him the £3 but he adamantly refused any extra for the shave and haircut. When I emerged ten minutes later, was feeling more confident about my interview.

There was a long trudge up a steep hill until I arrived at the drill hall where the interviews were to be held. There were at least a hundred, possibly two hundred men milling around inside. As I entered there was an announcement from a stentorian voice, "Number 1, Bombadier Hough!" Good God, I thought, I'm the first. A Regular Army Regimental Sergeant Major was at the door of the interview room, normally a terrifying figure, but this man was surprisingly calm and welcoming. "Good morning, son," he said, (what cheek I thought, son, he shouldn't be calling me son). I soon found he was a very kind man. "Now listen to me, son," he said, "When the president asks you what did you do, he does not want to know what was your civilian occupation. He is not the slightest bit interested. You are in the Army now. He wants to know what games you play and for God's sake don't say football. He will think you will mean soccer. He thinks gentlemen do not play soccer. They play rugby. If you are going to be an officer, you need to be a gentleman".

After entering I gave the president the smartest possible salute (longest way up, shortest down) and I was told to stand at ease and then easy. I must say the old buffer he did not look, or seem at all forbidding. He rather resembled the old caricature of Colonel Blimp. Florid face, white moustache tinged with ginger. He gave me a welcoming smile. His first question was,

"Well, what do you do, boy?" I was ready. I replied:

"My favourite game, Sir, is football. Rugby football." I hastened to add, "But as you can see my figure is slight, therefore I am useless in a scrum and as I am not particularly fleet of foot. I am equally useless as a three-quarter or a wing." (I thought this note of self-deprecation might at least partly assuage my lack of ability). "What else do you do, then?"

"Tennis, sir," I replied. "I was once selected to play for Cheshire in the National championships."

"Tennis! Tennis! Bloody girl's game!" (Not going well this, I thought, have to change my tack).

"I also am quite good at badminton." The president looked at his next adjacent colleague, whom I distinctly heard whisper, "It's a sort of garden ping-pong." I then felt things were going very badly, so hastily interceded with, "Squash, sir. A very tough and exhausting exercise."

"Don't know about that. It's another bloody girl's game!" said Blimp. I staggered on with the interview, doing, I thought, worse and worse and when, as a last, desperate inspiration came out with "Horse racing, Sir, Horse racing is my main sport and the only one I am any good at". The president looked up, leant forward and for the first time seemed to be taking a bit of interest. So did the rest of the panel.

"Horse racing? I suppose you mean point-to pointing?" That was true, but I felt no need to explain that my experience was limited to finishing third and last in a farmer's race. This was the time to trot out one of my favourite sayings, which had served me well in so many interviews:

"We all have to start somewhere", I said, with another slight self-deprecating smile. The inference could be taken to be, or was, that I had gone on to greater things. Like winning the Grand National. Even two Grand Nationals. Even three, who would know? Col. Blimp turned to his neighbour. I saw him mouth the words,

"Good chap, this. Just the type we need." A few days later I received written notification that I was to report to the OCTU (Officer Cadet Training Unit) at Llandrindrod Wells. Whoopee! So far I was through! There was another soldier's farewell for Pauline and then I left Scunthorpe forever. I was really sorry about this as I had a good time there.

HARDINGE'S BRIDGE

Hardinge was a viceroy of India during the thirties. The Bridge named after him was a cantilever construction crossing the river Ganges at one of its widest points at Pabna, then in India, later in East Pakistan, later still in Bangladesh. Pabna lay directly in the path of the Delhi Express from Calcuta. and the main lines to Imphal and Rangoon in Burma.

The bridge avoided lengthy rail detours. The Japs already had their eyes on the bridge as an entry point for their forthcoming invasion and conquest of India, widely considered on both sides to be inevitable and imminent.

De-training Guns at Hardinge's Bridge April 1943

Clearly it was of immense strategic importance and the man selected for its defence was me, an absurd appointment as I was the least qualified and youngest officer in the regiment having scraped through OCTU and emerged commissioned as a second lieutenant (eleven shillings a day.)

My unit in India was the 59th Light Anti-Aircraft Battery. Our armament at The Bridge consisted of ten Bofors 40mm automatic canons of which I had extensive experience in England. I had learned my trade as an artillery gunner with the 39th and also at OCTU. With extreme difficulty, due to the almost total absence of roads or even tracks in the locality, supplies were sent up from Calcutta daily by the Delhi Express. The train could not stop because of danger from dacoits (train robbers). Rations and other essentials were packed in basha hampers and flung off the train near the bridge and collected by us later. I do not recall any theft by locals or starving wild dogs. When all the guns were sited, in sandbagged emplacements, life could assume a modicum of normality. This being the army, we needed a headquarters, then an orderly room and, of course, for me, an officer's mess. As an officer and gentleman I was not expected to dine outside in the public gaze. A small settlement still existed at nearby Paxi, originally built to house the team in charge of building the bridge. These were still in situ as the builders had nowhere else to go. There were several basha bungalows and even a clubhouse. (Basha: the ubiquitous Indian building material of pliable dried palm fronds. Very strong, windproof, rotproof, rainproof and sunproof. And also a generic term for buildings of the material.) Contractors from Pabna erected other bashas for the mens'sleeping quarters etc.

Construction material for the bridge had been sent by train as far as possible and then manhandled to site by armies of men (and women). The rails and other heavy equipment went by rail as far as Pabna and then by a narrow gauge railway, specially built for the purpose, for the eight miles to Paxi through difficult jungle terrain now almost impenetrable after years of disuse.

There was no electricity on site and therefore no refrigeration. The Army sent us excellent quality beef, from Herefordshire cattle raised on fine grasslands in the Punjab and sent to Calcutta by refrigerated train. By the time it reached us it was almost inedible. This was causing wide dissent among the men and an early solution was required.

Sgt. Whittingham   **Sgt. Furlong**
See p.14   See p.14

I knew there was an ice factory at Pabna. It would be impossible for them to deliver (no roads) so the problem was how to get the ice from there to us. The only hope seemed to be the narrow gauge railway and somehow we must make it work again.

The locomotive, a small shunter, was still on the siding at Paxi, apparently complete but red with rust and in deplorable repair. The timber frames of the rolling stock had long since been smashed up for firewood. Only the useless bogey wheels remained. I had on my staff, as though a gift from God, Sergeant Whittingham, who before the war had been an artificer foreman at the Railway Locomotive Repair Workshops at Crewe. His inseparable mate was Sergeant Furlong whose civilian occupation had been cutting out a hundred suits at a time with Montague Burton, the fifty-shilling tailor. He knew nothing about railway engines but both set to work with a will to recusitate the Paxi-Pabna Railway. There was no shortage of volunteer help from off-duty gun teams. Sgt. Whittigham said that the boiler leaked like a colander and was so rotten it would die of fright if it saw a welding iron let alone have one applied to it. There was no way he could possibly repair it. The situation looked bleak. It looked like no engine, no ice. The leaks were all from the many joints between the steel plates, formed into a cylindrical shape, from which the boiler was constructed. One of our "think tank" on the job suggested that these could be sealed with china clay, on which the village of Paxi was built. This was immediately pooh-poohed on the grounds that clay would not stand the heat of the boiler. I had remembered reading that statues made of terracotta in Pompeii survived heats of 400deg.C. in the inferno which followed the eruption. The Oxford dictionary (never travel without one) told me terra cotta is a mixture of red china clay and sharp sand. Very quickly we had a terracotta factory in full production, managed by Sgt. Furlong. As a heatproof caulking agent it worked perfectly. Days later we were puffing into Pabna station with my large galvanised iron oval bath which made an excellent ice chest. The line had been cleared of fallen trees and undergrowth by a team of a hundred local ladies who were paid 4annas an hour. They liked the work because apart from the money they could go home with large bundles of free kindling on their heads. In India firewood is always expensive and in short supply, never used for cooking. Even in the poorest families, fresh chapattis are cooked daily on smouldering cow dung, neatly and lovingly patted into shape by hand. Consequently the fields are never fertilised and agricultural yields are low, the smell is appalling. Never venture into the Indian countryside at breakfast time.

KISTI AND THE BATTI WALLAH

Kisti was employed by me for most of my time in India. I met him at a transit camp soon after my arrival in Bombay when he was one of a large crowd of unemployed beavers all seeking work with the young British officers. They had learned that from the grapevine, which travels like a jumping jack in India that a bearing job was available and they were pushing, shoving shouting and thrusting chittis in my face. A chitti is a testimonial usually endorsing the holders integrity skill at waiting, writing, reading and valeting and signed by The Viceroy (often dead) and always a forgery produced by specialist suppliers in the local bazaar. One man stood alone and aloof at the back. He was very old but upright and fit-looking and wore a smart starched pugree (scarf headdress) and was observing the vulgarity of the crowd in front with undisguised disdain. When the mayhem died down I beckoned him over. He greeted me with both palms held together, in the Indian style, as though in prayer, and a smile. I asked him for his chitti. He produced one not only signed by the Viceroy but on embossed notepaper from the Viceregal Lodge indicating that it could have been genuine, though unlikely. It was signed "Curzon", i.e. Lord Curzon. I asked him how old he was. "Fifty, Sahib, was the reply. I could see he was at least seventy. "Thirty rupees a month plus rations", I said. From that moment on we were devoted friends. (Thirty rupees was 45/-. "Rations" was a hundredweight of atta, or coarse flour, for chapattis, rice, lentils, jugree (unrefined sugar) and other items obtainable by officers through M.E.S. for 20 rupees and enough to feed a family of five for a month. MES (Military

Engineering Services) ran the housing and catering side of the Army. Next day I was posted to a temporary assignment at Mhow, Central Provinces, as the outfit I was due to join in Calcutta had not yet assembled. I was given a first class railway warrant and off we went, Kisti, me and the luggage in a ghari (horse-drawn 4-wheel carriage), to Victoria Station. I realised would have to buy a ticket for Kisti, third class on backless wooden seats and very inexpensive. As I was queuing up at the ticket office Kisti came rushing up to me. "No, Sahib, me no need ticket". Well, that's a stroke of luck, I thought. I wonder why not. Maybe he gets it free as an old age pensioner. Kisti ordered the porter to stow my gear in the compartment aided by a tall lad of about 14 whom I had noticed hanging about with us several times before. Pointing to him, I asked Kisti who he was.

"Batti wallah, Sahib," he said.

"Kisti", I replied sternly. "I do not need a batti wallah. Tell him to go away."

"No, Sahib, you need batti wallah. All English gentlemen need batti wallah." The train was making ready-to-go noises.

"Kisti", I said, "tell him to clear off."

There was another officer sharing the compartment with me. As we sat down I asked him what the hell was a batti wallah? This chap was an old sweat who knew everything. He said that a batti wallah was a harijan, i.e. on the very bottom rung of the caste ladder, an untouchable, whose only possible task in the sum total of human endeavour was to fill and light the oil lamps at dusk every day.

"Is that all?" I said in some horror, "my bearer can do that."

"Oh, no he can't. Lighting oil lamps is a harijan's job. No bearer would touch it". I sank back into my seat thinking that if this was India I had better get used to it.

"You mean to tell me," I went on, "is all this lad does for a living is light a few oil lamps at night?"

"Oh, no, no. He turns them all off at dawn as well."

When we arrived at Mhow I was pleased to see a small group of porters with Kisti and Batti Wallah, who had promoted himself into the post of Assistant Baggage Master, striding confidently through the exit gate with a truck loaded with my luggage, (I was pleased to see him exit safely as he certainly would not have had a ticket. Kisti and Batti Wallah were strong believers in riding free on trains, on the roof). With him was my large black tin trunk, outsize vulcanised fibre expanding suitcase, two regulation Army kit bags, one canvas wash basin with soap pocket and folding stand plus a very large oval galvanised bath which we had somehow acquired along the way. "Sahib", said Batti Wallah, "these porters all very dam idle, need dam good kicking. I give them dam good kicking."

With that, he grabbed the nearest porter, turned him round, and, with his bare foot, treated him to a right fourpenny one, which, had he been a rugby ball, would have sent him flying over and through the goal posts.

I moved into very good accommodation with comfortable charpoys (rope beds) and mosquito nets shared with another new arrival. After dinner we would be at a loose end so I sent Kisti to find out what was on at the cinema in Mhow. Half an hour later he had not returned, so we went off to the mess and had a good dinner. An hour later there was a knock at our door. It was Kisti with Batti Wallah. They had been to the cinema but as neither could read English or Hindi they could not understand the posters or read what was showing. (It was Gone with the Wind, not yet released outside USA).

Therefore, displaying what I considered was commendable initiative, they had borrowed a jemmy or similar and wrenched the poster hoarding off the wall then wheeled it back to us on a borrowed hand cart.

As a reward for the enterprise, which I believed if of an unusually high order should always be rewarded, I gave Kisti the money for a chicken which he immediately eviscerated, cooked and ate with the Batti Wallah. A few days later Batti Walla appeared with a large, writhing snake which he was restraining with a strangulation hold. He said he had found it in my bed. I thanked him warmly but he showed no sign of moving on, clearly reckoning that it was worth another chicken. I stood my ground as this sort of racket would go on for ever unless stopped in the early stages I never knew if batti wallah had a name.

Kisti and Batti Wallah returning hoarding to cinema

I always addressed him as Batti Wallah and so did Kisti and everybody in the battery.

He did not seem to object.

ABDUL

A notice appeared on our board in the mess: "If any of you gentlemen play polo would be pleased to give you a game. Abdul Dewas, Maharajah". There was a telephone number so I rang it and spoke to a secretary. I explained that I had never played polo but as a cavalryman I could ride a horse and if there were such an event as a practice knockabout I would very much like to take part. I did not think it necessary to point out that I had been a mere trooper and not a cavalry officer. Maharajahs were always huge snobs in such matters.

Back, almost immediately, came a reply, delivered by runner." Come pig-sticking next Sunday. Pick you up at your Mess 7.am. If you cannot make it then do not bother to reply. No movement order had come through about Calcutta and the C.O. said in view of such a super invitation he would see that I would be excused all duties, if any, on Sunday. I immediately whizzed off to the bazaar on a bicycle I had hired and was measured up for new pair of jodhpurs and bought two white twill short sleeved shirts (6shillings each, lovely quality and I had them for years). With the topee crash hat (see cover, same one) I had already bought I reckoned I would be suitably togged up for the occasion.

The car, a 1939 Packard Sedan, turned up on time and I was driven off to the meet. I had accepted the invitation because I guessed I would be put on a super horse, would have an excellent lunch and I was right both times. The horse was a grey Arab stallion, about five years old. Absolutely superb. A gorgeous animal and a right handful but not beyond me. Arabs never geld their horses, I believe for religious reasons. How

27

would you like it? I had a wonderful morning cantering along in the rear of the main pack and saw a good few runs. I was carrying regulation six-foot lance, with sharpened and honed point, with which to spear a pig. I had no intention of spearing anything as I had always been anti-blood sports especially this cruellest and most violent of all.

Taus (HH Maharajah of Dewas) Mr. J Hough up, winner of central India Derby at Indore on Sunday.

Eventually it was lunch time and Abdul rode up. He dismounted and passed his horse to a syce, (groom) stretched out on my rug, propped his head up on his hand and said "Did not see much of you this morning! "Do you not know the old saying about valour and discretion not being good bedfellows?" I replied. A hoary and stale old cliche, but he put his head back and roared with laughter. He said it was a wise attitude, especially first time. A bearer was passing round drinks and Abdul insisted I try an arak nimbu pani, a concoction new to me, of double distilled palm oil i.e.(liquid gunpowder) and fresh lime juice. I was also pressed to try his very own Dewas pork pie. I could not help thinking that the poor animal who provided it was probably speared only yesterday. It was delicious, even better than the product famously made by Carters of Warrington, which my family always patronised on the way home from Haydock Park Races.

Abdul was in an expansive mood. He sat quite a long time with me, chatting about one thing and another. Eventually he paused and said, "Look here, you don't play polo, you're useless at pig-sticking and you don't play cricket. What the hell do you do?" I did not want to say nothing. I wanted to get on that horse again and have another of those lunches. So I said, "Horse-racing."

"Horse-racing? I suppose you mean pointing", said Abdul (he had asked me to address him thus), somewhat derogatorily. Out it came again.

"We all have to start somewhere", I said smiling, inferring, but not saying, that I had gone on to greater things. No point in lying at this stage.

"And whereabouts?" he asked.

"Cheshire, chiefly", I said. The race in which I had finished third and last was because the horse had decanted me before the last jump, then turned round and jumped it alone, then kindly stopped while a spectator assisted me to remount and I finished third and last. Until then this had been the sole athletic achievement of any sort whatsoever in my entire life.

Abdul asked me where else I had ridden and I replied, "France, Belgium, South Africa and other countries", which was perfectly true but not in races. I had merely been asked where I had ridden and I had truthfully answered the question. He seemed impressed and suddenly said to me that I could be just the chap he was looking for.

"I have a very good horse called Taus", he said, "who is currently favourite for the Central India Derby at Indore next Sunday which, as you know, is the biggest race for G.R.'s (Gentleman Riders or amateurs) in India. The man I engaged to ride him cannot come because he is detained in Burma, could you possibly take the mount for me?" I knew it would be a massive opportunity and a huge thrill but everything was wrong. I was not racing fit, was almost certainly overweight and had equally certainly given him an impression of my ability well above the actual which was fairly slight. He did not pause to consider this. He said that he was delighted and that was a deal and he would have me picked up at 8am on Sunday morning.

Indore races is a popular festival and at least twenty thousand spectators were present. I soon learned that the

Maharajah would not be present as he was detained elsewhere. In the weighing room I met the trainer who gave me the silks and helped me weigh out at 8 st. 10. The saddle weighed under a pound. The man was useless with his advice and merely told me that Taus (pronounced Ta-oos), was a good horse, which I already knew, and should not give me any trouble. I should jump off about third or fourth, ease him into the lead at the distance and go on to win easily.

I do not normally suffer from nerves but I was now beginning to feel as I felt when that German sharp shooter was having a go at me at North Coates. I was introduced to a Major Percival, a first class rider who was in the Irish army and riding another fancied horse in the race (which had international pretensions) I told him that I was unfit and I was terrified that I might be carted (bolted with) on the way to the start, (the ultimate shame.) He said not to worry. He knew how I felt, he often felt the same. He would give me a lead and we would take a slow canter. After mounting we trotted our horses past the grandstand where there was a row of bookmakers shouting the odds. Surprisingly, in English. (Later in life I was to learn that in whatever country one might be racing, it would always be conducted in English). The bookies were shouting "Take two to one Taus!" Good God, I thought. I'm odds on. "Could that be right?" I said to Percival? "Favourite 2-1 on?" "You're right", said Percival. "But remember that this is a very tough crowd and if you don't win they'll have you off that horse. Maybe a lynching party." I thought this a poor taste joke.

Those who have never been astride a blood horse would not realise that it can accelerate from the standing position to 35mph in five strides. Unless one's feet are correctly stirrupped there is a distinct likelihood that an inexperienced rider, not quite ready, might ignominiously slide off backwards. I did not want this to happen to me. I was ready for it and it did not happen. The horse and I jumped off well and I was soon aware that I might be considerably in front. I did not want to look round as it might unbalance the horse. But, turning into the straight, second and last time round, I risked glancing back. To my amazement I could not see another horse. I was at least a half a furlong in front. For the first time I felt totally relaxed and really enjoying myself. I had all the time in the world to sort myself out look as much like Gordon Richards (the champion jockey) as possible and pass the winning post in front of all the other horses and the photographers. If I could not play the part I could at least, I thought, look it.

It was now late 1943 and obvious to everybody in our army that the Japanese air force no longer posed a threat to Hardinge's Bridge or any other strategic target in India. The 59th L.A.A Regiment was hastily wound down and its officers and men transferred to other arms of the service where they would be more use. It became our lot to find ourselves no longer skilled artillerymen but untrained infantry soldiers of the 4th battalion the Queen's Royal Regiment, a territorial unit raised and based at Guildford, (later at Gravesend) whose famous Chindit columns of the 14th Army in Burma had been severely depleted by casualties, Malaria, dengue fever, beri beriberi and various other disasters. We were raw reinforcements and immediately hurled into a rigorous regime of preparatory training, mostly involving extreme forms of exercise, danger from live ammunition and semi-starvation diet (No use to me now. Race-riding and the need for weight reduction was finished). A start was made with replacing our hopelessly out-dated clothing and equipment. Out went our absurd Boy Scout felt hats which repelled neither rain nor sun. In, as a gift from the US army, came a bale of 100 lightweight trilbies, apparently indestructible and made of a magical new material nobody had heard of, fibreglass. When not in use the hats folded up and slipped into a pocket. We were so delighted. Accompanying them was note saying we were not to waste time with acknowledgement or thanks but if we wanted some more we had only to say so. This was typical of the generosity and thoughtfulness frequently extended to us by the Americans.

Battledress was scrapped in favour of lightweight one-piece boiler suits. New, well-made boots made in South Africa were provided. Chindit troops in Burma were still at the mercy of brainless ordnance bods in Whitehall who lumbered us with outdated equipment from the Boer and Great wars merely to save money. Among the most monstrous were our back packs, made of heavy webbing material with solid brass buckles and fittings which shone brightly in the sunlight, greatly helping the aim of Jap snipers. Eventually these were replaced with by light weight Bergen rucksacks, much loved by modern mountaineers and hikers. These were supported on the body by shoulder straps and also metal frames which rested on the hip bones thereby giving them jaundice, i.e. black and blue from bruising.) Not much could be done with other heavy equipment like water bottles and ground sheets, as plastics had not yet been invented. Fully loaded with essentials, the Bergen weighed about 25lb. Its Boer War predecessor similarly laden was 40lb.

POSTSCRIPT: At the time of writing these notes Britain was engaged in a protracted war in Afghanistan. From accounts I read our men's efforts there were constantly hampered by obsolete, inadequate, unsuitable equipment supplied by idiots in Whitehall. Nothing much changes.

At the end of the flat racing season in India, in the monsoon period, racing took place at some tracks on a cinder course. The cinders were extracted from the boilers of the big clothing factories, then granulated into a shrapnel like material which made a perfect safe galloping surface. It was, though, unpleasant to gallop through, both for horse and rider. I was asked to ride a horse called Lotus in an amateur hurdle race at Mahalaxmi. It belonged to a lady, Jane Shufflebottom, daughter of a prominent racehorse owner and mill owner in Bombay. The horse had not done much, but on the other hand nor had I, as I had never ridden over hurdles so was pleased to get the chance.

It is possible to get a very good idea of a horse's intentions during a race by watching his ears. The ears tell you everything. If they move gradually to and fro, you know he is reasonably happy about the proceedings. If the ears go back, he is profoundly unhappy and will either slow up or refuse at the next jump. If he waggles his ears side to side, that is an indication that he has not made his mind up about what he is to do next. As we approach the first hurdle, Lotus moved his ears side to side. I knew, in spite of the flying cinders, that he had not seen the obstacle and he galloped on resolutely, straight through it. I do not remember much about what happened thereafter except that I woke up in the Victoria hospital, Bombay, with severe concussion and a fractured foot. At the foot of the bed there was Mr Boulton in his jodhpurs and black leggings. I could hear somebody saying I was delirious. He was wagging his forefinger at me, "The number of times I've told you not to ride a horse into a hurdle on a lateral reign, and what do you do? You do just that! And what happens? The horse falls! You lost the race Jim, lad, not good!" Miss Shufflebottom brought me a box of fudge.(Note: Mr Boulton was head lad at the racing stables of B.M. Bullock, Delamere Forest, and taught me to ride racehorses there between the ages of 10 and 17).

THE TURF CLUB

As a result of my foot injury I missed my boat home and was given accommodation in a luxurious furnished bungalow in Poona, while waiting for a week or two for the next voyage home. Poona. What a treat. Great town, great racecourse and a great and famous club, The Turf.

All social life with the Raj in India evolved round the Clubs, which were in every large town. These establishments were luxurious, fairly inexpensive and served superb food. Admission was strictly members only and to become a member was a lengthy and laborious procedure. To an Indian, almost impossible unless of royal rank (e.g. Maharajah) or qualified amateur rider, or bearer of an English title. Lord Willingdon. who was Viceroy in, I think, 1937, was so disgusted with this aspect of the colour bar that he promoted a new club for Bombay, later called The Willingdon, to which membership was available to everybody, regardless of status or colour. Until then, the only people granted immediate free admission were serving officers, who, if in uniform, were made honoury members on the spot. In those day all officers were assumed to be gentlemen, a dictum which would not obtain today. The one exception to this rule was The Turf Club. There, in addition to being a serving officer, further proof were needed for status as a gentleman before memberships were granted. This was easy for me as I was an accepted and official listed "G.R.", i.e. gentleman rider. At the time I found it mildly amusing that my commanding officer, a Lieutenant Colonel, and socially the most delightful man one could wish to meet, was denied honoury membership. I had to sign him in. I warned him he should not expect future favours of this nature from me unless he behaved himself. He would need to watch his table manners!

On my first day at Poona, with my foot in plaster, I stumped along to the Turf in good time for lunch, and was introduced by the barman to a Parsee who,in his youth, had also been a G.R. He bought me a drink and asked if I would care for a game of snooker. I am the world's worst player but it would pass the time so I said yes. "Five chips all right?" This was 7s.6d., not a lot but I had to watch the money. I had a stay in Poona to finance plus a voyage home. I need not have worried. I was not the world's worst snooker player. He was. I knew this when he asked would I mind if he used the blunt end of the cue. I won, and like the gentleman he was, he stumped up the five chips which financed a return round of drinks and my lunch.

He was there again the next day and I could see he was still smarting from having been beaten by somebody was a patently worse player than even him. That was another five chips.

PANDIT NEHRU
AND INDIRA GANDHI

On Saturday nights there was often a dinner-dance, with some topical European dance music, excellently performed by an all-Indian orchestra. They played songs from Oklahoma, over and over again, which then had not then been heard anywhere outside USA and the tunes were something of a craze. I was often invited to join Nehru's table as I was a useful dancing partner for Indira. Nehru was always extremely polite and entertaining to me. He seemed not to be overtly anti-British. In fact he admired, he said, our administrative abilities. Neither he nor Indira was any way related to Mahatma Gandhi. They dined at the Turf because they preferred the food there to Indian food. Nehru was engaged in an ongoing affair with Lady Edwina Mountbatten, wife of the Viceroy, which was the subject of much twittering. I never saw the two together.

It was a huge privilege for me to know Indira, a brilliantly attractive, entertaining, clever and witty woman. She was four years older than me. The story of her life was almost unbelievable. She became India's first prime minister in 1967. Shortly after assuming power she declared a state of National Emergency after a High Court ruling found her guilty of electoral fraud. Meanwhile her son, Sanjay, with Indira's help, had assumed control and started to run the country as though it was his personal property and was intensely disliked. In an attempt to curb rampant population growth he initiated a programme of enforced sterilisation. Because of widespread unrest she called for fresh elections but she herself was trounced at the polls. Three years later she was to return yet again as prime minister. Sanjay was killed in an air crash in 1977. Mistakenly confident that she had regained the trust of the nation after India's triumph in the war against Pakistan she again tried for the top job but was yet again indicted for illegal electoral practices and again found guilty. That was effectively the end of Indira, by far the most remarkable, cleverest, and entertaining person I have known.

She once told me she had learned The Twist at Oxford and in the midst of a demonstration which I had requested, I accidentally trod on a hem of her sari which slipped to the floor and exposed two totally naked shoulders and unhealed inoculation scars on her upper arm.

Her father, Pandit Nehru, was leader of the Indian National Congress party which was committed to expelling the British so that they could govern their country themselves. All the British thought they were incompetent to do so. Many of the educated classes of Indians agreed possibly including, secretly, Nehru. Indira could not understand my fondness of horse-racing which she considered an inconsequential, uninteresting and worthless pursuit. In spite of that, we got on well together. She and the Pandit always addressed me as Mr Hough rather than Jim. I called her Indhira and her father Pandit.

"Pandit" is a courtesy title meaning "learned man." (In the Hindi style the word Pandit is pronounced half way between 'Pandit and Pundit). He usually had a few words with me at the table and was always extremely entertaining and polite. At heart, I believed, he was pro-British and admirer of our administration. He was apparently on very friendly terms with Lady (Edwina) Mountbatten, the Viceroy's wife. Although whispers abounded I never saw Nehru with her at the Club. I did my duty by Indhira and although an appallingly bad ballroom dancer often had a dance or two with her. That was why I was included in their table.

In 1967, when known as Indira Gandhi, she became the first woman prime minister in India. She was not related to Mahatma Gandhi but on her return to India from Oxford in 1965 had married another man of that name, Feroze Ghandi, a young intellectual Parsee who was also no relation to the famous Gandhi. He died in 1960. She had an extensive education in English at Somerville College, Oxford, Poona University and also in Hindi (Indo-Germanic language of the Hindus) at an educational establishment in India founded by Rabinranath Tagore, the renowned Hindi sceptic and poet.

I asked her what she had learned of value at Oxford and what had proved the most use and given her the greatest pleasure. She replied, unhesitatingly, "The Twist." I asked her to give me a 'dem' and she immediately leaped to her feet, and pulled me up beside her. I was a total failure at the Twist and trod on the hem of her sari which dropped to the floor exposing her two totally bare shoulders and two unhealed inoculation scars, singularly unexciting. She became the first woman prime minister of India in 1967. Shortly afterwards a state of national emergency was declared after the High Court found her guilty of electoral fraud.

By 1973, again prime minister, she was racked by demonstrations against her and was yet again forced to resign. She was now finished in the big time. She had gone too far. She never rose again and died in 1974, wickedly and cruelly assassinated by two of her own bodyguards.

Indira was four years older than me. She was brilliantly clever and sometimes highly amusing but we had almost nothing in common. I believe she enjoyed our evenings together at the Turf because of the good English food and the fact that I was not a social climber who would hassle her and introduce her to people she did not want to meet. She could not understand my interest in horse-racing which she considered dull and inconsequential.

JOHN TAYLOR
<u>AND FIVE ROSES TEA</u>

I met John soon after arrival at Durban in 1942. I was at a tented transit camp at Clairwood, on the outskirts, awaiting further orders and transport. None had come through so I was given the remainder of the day off and told to report again the following day. This might have been my one and only day in South Africa so I wanted to see at least a bit of it and decided on a walk, along the main road, through huge sugar plantations. I did not know that sugar grew on tall, hairy sticks. I though it grew in cubes. (No, I didn't.) A car stopped. The driver was John Taylor and he offered me a lift. I said I had just arrived and was going nowhere in particular.

"In that case," he said, "come to my home, meet my wife and family and have a cup of tea. I live just down the road."

Of course I said yes. His house, a pleasant little bungalow, had pineapples, grapes and apples growing in the garden. The cost, he said, including the use of two servants, was £5 a week. His pay as a bank clerk was also £5 a week. This did not sound quite right to me so I asked him what did he live on? That, he explained, was the beauty of South Africa. It was so easy to make money on the side. The whole country abounded in opportunities. He had a used car lot, a tea blending business and a few other enterprises, all costing nothing to start but already making good money. They included a baking powder business which was made with useless grape pip mush discarded from wineries. (I did not believe this last one but made a mental note to go into it further) Jim, he said, when you get home, get out of the army as fast as you possibly can and come straight back here. You will be mad if you do not. That's if you want to make money. Unlike all those other layabouts back home. And what, I asked, do I use for money? Money! MONEY! *MONEY!* Money grows on trees in South Africa.Like the apples. You just borrow it. Any bank will throw money at you if you just have half an idea. I could introduce you to mine. The trouble is, John, I said, that I do not really have any ideas.

Jim, nobody likes to hear those negative thoughts. Think positive. Be positive. I am positive, I said. But, John, just give me one idea. You live here. I don't. OK, said John. How about this? There is nobody. Nobody, can you believe it, in the whole of South Africa making potato crisps! Nobody! That's hardly surprising, I said. The Bantus, Kaffirs Zulus and the other Negroid races do not eat potatoes. They eat mealies and almost nothing else. THEN MAKE THEM EAT BLOODY POTATOES! replied John.

Jim, he added, I cannot put up with any more of your defeatistim. I am beginning to think you are not the type we want out here. I thought you were, but it seems you are not. What about the huge white population who like potato crisps? OK, I said, but I would not know how to start and get going.

Jim, said John, I keep telling you do not need to know. You pick it up as you go along. That's what I do.

I still don't like it much, I said. Any other businesses you have thought of?

Yes, said John. Listen to this. There is nobody in the entire continent of Africa, the entire huge continent, not a single, solitary person, making hair cream. It is a wide open, unexploited market. Anybody's for the taking.

That, I said, is hardly surprising. Zulus and Bantus, with hair like theirs, would never use hair cream. Even a shovelful of Brylcreem could not keep it down. I could have guessed his reply: THEN MAKE 'EM USE BLOODY HAIR CREAM!

We did not fall out over this. Far from it. John regarded me as a difficult, but not impossible, subject who required further coaching in the desirability of returning to South Africa after the war He was convinced that there could be no real prosperity there until the whites outnumbered the blacks and he earnestly believed this was possible.

I told him that I would probably have another day off on the following day and I would know by 8am. He said if I would like to see more of his business enterprises, to give me more ideas, he would pick me up at 8.15. If I was not there he would know I could not come.

I did have another free day and John was waiting at the gate. We whizzed off in his car to a small shanty town just outside Durban. It was just a ragbag collection of tumbledown dwellings made of cardboard, rusty corrugated iron, old advertisement hoardings and anything which might help to keep some rain and all the sun out. There was just one building, right in the middle of this shambolic slum, which was different. It was about 40 feet tall, though only one brick thick (no possible merit in two bricks thick, said John; No safer and a waste of money). There was no staircase, I was told, but two rope ladders ran up each of the four sides and down the whole of the front, covering four or five floors, there was an enormous flashing, red neon sign comprising letters about five feet wide and four feet high. They read: FIVE ROSES TEA. At night it would have lit up the sky for miles. Beneath that, to drive the point home were five depictions of red roses, also flashing.

There you are, Jim, said John, proudly. And I can tell you that sign cost more than the entire building, including the land! Africa's first tea blender. That's me!

It was not a state of the art modern production plant but John described in some detail and with considerable, pride, how it worked.

Teams of local ladies, each with a sack of tea, (Assam, Kenyan, Rhodesian and other varieties over a shoulder, climbed the ladders and tipped the contents into a large hopper at the top. Amazingly, said John, It all floats down to the bottom without mechanical motivation, entirely free of charge and relying entirely on gravity (I could have guessed that) on to a large trestle table. Other ladies scooped it up and shovelled it into various coloured packets. It all blends together, John explained, as it floats down in whatever proportions we consider appropriate, usually involving cost and availability. Notice that there is no expensive machinery. The ladies can be trained to do this work very quickly. Economy and efficiency is the secret of a good business. Do not forget that when you come here to join us and make your own fortune. You will need a car. And don't forget to buy it only from me he added.

Twenty years later I was at a party in Cobham, Surrey, where I lived and was introduced to a man who told me he had just retired as Chief of Police in Durban. I told him I was there during the War and what a lovely town I thought it was. Not today it isn't, he said. It's not the same today. Ruined by thoughtless and tasteless over-development So many people have told me that about Durban. What a shame.

I asked him had he heard of a firm called Five Roses Tea. Of course, he replied. Five Roses Tea runs Africa. They are into everything. Shopping malls, hotel chains, newspapers, film production, car and truck assembly and they are just about to start their own clearing bank. Why do you ask? I said that I had met the founder, John Taylor, when in Durban and I was pleased to hear that he had apparently succeeded in life. I thanked him for his time. On the way out, as the party was ending, he was involved with another group, but I had forgotten to ask him one important question.

So sorry to bother you again, I said, butting in, do you know if Five Roses Tea make, or ever made, hair cream? No idea was the reply. But if there is money in it you can bet your life they did.

There were only two components of the British rations. There was a cube of dried compressed oatmeal which the men called "bourgee", a type of porridge. Also a packet of ten "Victory V" cigarettes. Almost all soldiers smoked in those days. These were made in India of almost unbelievably poor quality. They were harsh in taste and would not stay alight until the end of the fag, perhaps just as well, twig and bound with cotton.

It was a relief when the Australians started victualing us. They, unlike the other great powers, inaugurated air drops by parachute. It was not a Chindit practice to plod along in the wide open spaces so the Aussies sometimes had trouble finding us. When they did, the chutes stuck in the tops of trees, or if there were a breeze, drifted for miles before dropping to earth, perhaps by then in another country. The Aussies therefore stopped drops by parachutes (much to the dismay of local natives, who had converted many of them into clothing and tents), and substituted loose drops. Rations were chucked out of the plane loose from a height of a few hundred feet or more and we found and recovered them when we could. We were able to communicate with the drop planes by walkie-talkie which had a range of about a mile. We were able to tell them how much we appreciated the small tins of pear segments and pineapple we had received. Australians are generosity personified and on the next drop we were alarmed to find 7lb.tins of Del Monte cling peaches in their own syrup and pineapple chunks being flung at us. Fortunately they missed.

Then the Americans took over the task of feeding us and again life changed for the better. I remarked to one of the American officers I met how much I admired his hat, which was similar to the one I had seen Frank Sinatra wearing in pictures. He told me it was made of a completely new material called fibreglass and was virtually indestructible, fireproof and repelled both rain and sun. As an added advantage it folded up into a very small space and slipped into pocket when not in use. I said that compared with the absurd gear we had to wear it was a superb hat. Immediately this man said, "How many do you want?" I was not expected to be given any but he said "would a hundred be enough?" I did not need anything like one hundred for my men but they could easily be absorbed by the other column. Next day, delivered by jeep, a bale of these super hats arrived and for a short time I was very popular!

Along with the Americans came their famous 'K' rations which were to become widely appreciated in all the allied forces,. Anybody that lived on 'K' rations for three months or more, like me, would recall, with extreme clarity, their exact contents, which were: for breakfast, (for instance) scrambled egg with chopped ham. This was packed in foil tins of about two inches radius, only about a teaspoonful but when placed in water immediately swelled up to about ten times the size. After the food we had been accustomed to this made a tasty and nutritious change.

In the same type of pack, contained in a box about six inches long and one inch deep, which had been sealed with candle grease or similar covering which protected the box from weather and rivers when had to wade through them, were a variety of entrées and desserts for other meals. These included steak and kidney pudding, roast chicken with vegetables, plum duff and custard and rice pudding. To complete the rations for one day there would be five sticks of Wrigley's spearmint chewing gum, five packets of instant coffee, five tea bags (then totally unknown in Europe), sugar, water purification tablets and a packet of four Chesterfield cigarettes (or sometimes Camel or Lucky Strike) and matches. Also five sheets of lavatory paper which was a bit on the stingy side.

On one occasion, I was saddled with a squad of about ten West African soldiers. These were splendid men but totally unused to Western habits. 'K' rations totally baffled them. I went along to see them at dinner time, to see how they were getting along and was amazed to find that they had emptied the entire contents of the 'K' pack, excluding the lavatory paper, into a dixie of boiling water and were stirring vigorously. The chewing gum and Nescafe were added, all bubbling away merrily.

We needed to be re-clothed, re-shod and re-equipped It still makes me quake with anger when I think of the useless, antiquated equipment, some mothballed since the Boer and Great wars, that our useless Ordnance bodes in Whitehall saddled us with in India, Assam and Burma just to save a miserable few pounds. A dreadful example was the back pack, made of heavy webbing material and weighing, empty, 12lb. It did not repel rain but had to carry our spare clothing, rubberised groundsheet (v. heavy, 7lb.,one week's rations (also 7lb) some small arms ammunition and other vital items.

Buckles and other fittings were of solid brass, the heaviest material available, which still needed to be polished for Sunday kit inspections, reflected the sunlight and were much appreciated by Japanese snipers in the trees, who could spot us from a mile away. It was replaced by a light weight Bergen Rucksack which had been sold by Millet's very cheaply for years and was standard equipment for hikers and mountaineers. (Note: The Army did not part with one of these unless the old Boer War version was handed in, presumably for mothballing until the next war). Water bottles and groundsheets today are of polythene or other lightweight plastics which in those days had not been invented. The Allied Armed forces (in Burma, Britain, Australia and USA), took it in turns to supply our rations. Guess which were the worst. You are right. Britain, by far. Mainstay of the British contribution was hard tack biscuits, in appearance much like dog biscuits. They were so hard that normal teeth could not dissect them so it is not possible to comment on their flavour. All we do know is that when they were offered to starving whelps in the villages they would take one sniff and bolt in terror. Our mules also refused to try them, even when granulated with heavy stones. The biscuits, (not the mules). The disgusting smell of these biscuits was because they were stuffed with synthetic vitamins of supposedly nourishing and health-giving properties. Orde Wingate, the Chief Chindit, said they would be useful in encouraging bowel movements. This was the man who strode along jungle paths carrying the Holy Bible in one hand and in the other Jane's Journal, a strip cartoon compendium of the the life of a scantily clad adventuress from the Daily Mirror. In any other society he would have been arrested or certified or both.

There were only two other components of the British rations. There was a large cube of dried compressed oatmeal which the men called" bourgee", a type of porridge. Also a packet of ten "Victory V" cigarettes. Almost all soldiers smoked in those days. These were made in India of almost unbelievably poor quality. Their flavour reminded me of those we manufactured ourselves at prep school and had the harsh taste of dead beech leaves rolled in blotting paper. They cured me of smoking for ever. A booklet of matches was provided, never enough but some men became adept at bisecting these with a razor blade to double the quantity and then reinforcing with a suitable twig and bound together with cotton.

It was a relief when the Australians started victualing us. They, unlike the other Allied powers, inaugurated air drops by parachute. It was not a Chindit practice to plod along in the wide open spaces so the Aussies sometimes had trouble finding us. When they did, the chutes stuck in the tops of trees, or if there were a breeze, drifted for miles before dropping to earth, perhaps by then in another country. The Aussies therefore stopped parachutes (much to the dismay of local natives, who had many of them), and swiftly converted them to clothing and tents and substituted loose drops. Rations were chucked out of the plane loose from a height of a few hundred feet or more and we found and recovered them when we could. We were able to communicate with the drop planes by walkie-talkie which had a range of about a mile. We told them how much we appreciated the small tins of pear segments and pineapple we had received. Australians are generosity personified and on the next drop we were alarmed to find 7lb.tins of Del Monte cling peaches and pineapple chunks being flung at us. Fortunately they missed.

It was sometimes possible to buy food by local purchase. In view of the Army's paranoia about all forms of money, particularly cash, it will surprise many to learn that officers were given a hundred Indian rupees a day (then £7.10s) to buy what they could in the villages It was also to be used for buying information, invariably false or useless. When it had all gone one only had to ask for more and, unbelievably, no receipts or accounts were required. The locals were extremely cautious about dealing with us as they had been diddled by the Japs and their fake money. There seemed to be no Burmese currency in circulation. They all knew what Indian money was worth. Victory "Vs, our loathsome cigarettes, were highly prized and we could usually get a small, scraggy chicken, about the size of a healthy blackbird, as a straight swap for a packet of 10. Larger birds, a pound weight or a bit more, would cost about five chips (7s6d.). One had to remember that these people were extremely short of food themselves. Still, they did not want to know about our British biscuits, even as a gift. Small goats, which taste remarkably like mutton, were also available as were tomatoes but these, apart from being red, bore no resemblance whatsoever to English tomatoes. They were totally tasteless and did not even smell of tomatoes. Securing live goats or chickens did not always solve food problems. Although every man in our unit would, given a chance, shoot a Jap soldier dead without a moment's second thought there was not a single man in our unit willing to dispatch a chicken or a goat.

An agreeable addition to our diet was fresh marshmallows. These should not be confused with the pastel coloured glutinous sweetmeats dusted with sieved icing sugar. They are small cantaloupe melons, about the size of walnuts, which grow freely in grassy, marshland in N Burma, very sweet and juicy. They are the only wild foodstuff which is indigenous to Burma. Consumption of a hatful at one sitting is inadvisable.

A story had reached my ears that the CO of our adjoining column, also part of the Queen's, was about to reach his 50th birthday. Fifty is a ripe old age for a Chindit but this man was very fit. He was also an extremely capable commander and well liked by all ranks in the regiment. His brother officers decided that the event called for a celebration well beyond the confines of "K" rations, scrawny chickens and badly-cooked goats.

Contact with the world outside one's column in those days was difficult and theoretically impossible. It can be reasonably supposed that it is now too late for institution of proceedings under Military Law for the events which followed but one can never be sure in the Army and readers are therefore asked to keep it all to themselves.

The Column could make contact with Regimental headquarters by walkie-talkie. Further contact could be possible with the Indian National Telephone Network in but only in circumstances of extreme and dire urgency. Such a call was made to Firpo's Restaurant in Calcutta. Firpo's was the best restaurant in Calcutta and probably the whole of India. The Maitre d' was Mr Resinelli, an Italian who had a dual function as a highly successful amateur jockey. He had been leading rider at Tollyunge, a Racing Club in Calcutta, for many years before and after this event. He was on friendly terms with the author of these notes. Mr Resinelli was asked to prepare a deluxe 4-course meal for six people for which the circumstances were explained, packed in strong and non-returnable containers. Reheating could be effected on site. Composition of the meal would be left to him. Everything was to be of the very choicest possible quality, regardless of expense. It would be collected on the day of the birthday. Somebody would call in to settle next month. The good signor said that nobody need call. It would not be necessary as Firpo's would be honoured to supply everything with their compliments.

All went well. It could not have been better. On the day of the birthday the drop pilot, a young Flying Officer, probably not much more than 20, from the Australian Air Force, collected the food himself from Firpo's, took it to Alipore Air

Field (just outside Calcutta), took off, flew to the drop zone then made an accurate delivery by parachute. The dinner, plus two bottles of Nasik Whisky thrown in by kind Mr Resinelli, was a resounding success.

Fame is seldom immortal and it is sad to relate that Firpo's no longer exists.

We had been told, frequently, until we were all sick of it, that the Japanese soldier could march for thirty miles a day with a 40lb. pack on his back on only a handful of rice and no sleep. Further, he would stand and fight to the last man, and to the last bullet and willingly die for his King Emperor. The truth of the matter was less heroic. The Jap soldier was yellow through and through, and not only his skin. At the first sign of real danger we had seen that he could bunk off as fast as the next man, or faster. Their failure to stand and fight at the Rupee Cash ambush (see [page 1) was one of the triggers which set off a mass Japanese defection and desertion. The Jap army or what was left of it, then set off on foot for the 600 mile slog to Rangoon, a few miles to the north of which they had already set up a base camp and a substantial redoubt. They would have to walk most of the way because they had little motorised transport. Had they persuaded the Burmese to take them by train, the Chindits, for sure, would have blown up the railway line. The Burma Road, as a highway, was still incomplete and much of it impassable. (Note: 14th Army Chindits had now been operating 500 miles behind the Jap lines for at least a year).

The task of the Japanese Army now looked hopeless but it seemed to us that they would not yet throw in the sponge. Our army had to face the grim reality of yet another seaborne invasion, this time from India to the west coast of Burma, involving a journey of 1,600 miles. And here we were hoping the war was nearly over. Some hope!

At this point it is expedient to explain why the Japanese had so little motorised transport. It had not all been wrecked in ambushes. Far from it. Our men took pains to try to capture it intact. They often succeeded and regarded such vehicles as prizes of war and therefore their personal property and potentially nice little earners as buses on the streets of Calcutta (of which there was an extreme shortage). A Jap vehicle similar to our 15cwt. pick-up truck could, in Calcutta, with a squash, easily accommodate 30 paying passengers. It would be a tight fit. But what do they expect for a few annas? Small complications needed to be overcome such as finding safe harbours in or near the villages until there was a convenient and expedient time to collect the trucks. These were not beyond the ingenuity of your average Chindit. He would patiently explain to the locals that the captured Jap vehicles were the property of The King of England who was a very powerful man and extremely unforgiving to those who displeased him. Nobody, if he had any sense, should risk this displeasure which could, for instance, be instantly invoked by the theft of a sparking plug, a crime which would warrant the ultimate penalty, death by hanging.

ELEPHANTA ISLE

My Sybaritic life in the fleshpots of Poona came to a sudden end when, early one morning, a dispatch rider on an American speed cop's high-powered Indian motor cycle, with high handlebars, fishtail exhausts (to add to the noise) and flashing headlights zoomed into my drive and slithered into a perfectly executed stem Christy stop adjacent and parallel to my front door. I do like a bit of style. This was style at its very best. The rider could access my door knocker without rising from his seat. I could see from the mudguard markings that he was from Division. This set my alarm bells ringing. Division did not correspond with junior officers through dispatch riders. It would normally be via the usual channels, that is brigade, regiment battalion column and company. This must be something urgent, perhaps unpleasantly so. Maybe the Firpo's dinner drop and its attendant misuse of aviation fuel. Surely nobody would be mean enough to put the squeak in about that. It couldn't be the Calcutta bus scam. The people who managed it were right at the pinnacle of the Calcutta Mafia, and they had not attained that high status without being sensible, reliable and utterly trustworthy men who behaved with total and unquestioned propriety Questions could be asked about some other perhaps slightly dubious matters but at that very early hour I could not imagine what they might be. So it was with some trepidation that I opened the buff envelope marked "Most Secret" (a security classification new to me although all pretences of secrecy, at this stage of the war, had virtually ceased. Everybody in Bombay knew what we were up to in Elephanta and was not the slightest bit interested). A hope lingered that it might contain my ticket home on Monarch of Bermuda and I could now see if they had given me a decent cabin and second sitting for dinner. There was no ticket home and it was to emerge later that this, and my demobilization, were indefinitely postponed. (For a year). The envelope contained Regimental Daily and Part 2 Orders and Divisional Orders. Daily Orders concerned only the usual boring daily business. Nothing to be worried about there. Divisional Orders Part 2 was more administrative matters of postings and so on. Right at the bottom, as the final item, was the news that Lieut. H.J. Hough had been promoted to the rank of Acting Captain with the additional post of Head of Waterproofing (whatever that might be) with immediate effect. Capt. Hough was to report to the R.T.O. at Poona for travel arrangements to Elephanta Isle. Captain was all right. Fifteen bob a day, in fact quite good. I did not like "Acting". This was to be expected. Only Regular officers held substantive ranks, i.e. permanent. "Acting" ranks finished when the War did, which might be quite soon. "Acting" ranks wore the same badges of rank, and held the exactly same responsibilities, as substantives. The difference was that as soon as the War ended "Acting" ranks reverted to their previous lower rank and pay thereof. The beauty of this scheme to the Army was that it saved them huge sums of money in lower demobilisation gratuities. This was widely considered to be a disgustingly dirty trick. We did not want to be in their sodding army. We joined it to save the world from the joint scourges of Hitler and the Rising Sun. And this is all he thanks we get. Bloody lot. If there is a next war they can stuff it.

I had decided not to take Kisti and Batti Wallah to Elephanta with me as there was no indication how long that stint might last which might cause complications for them. A good racing friend of mine was Mess Secretary at Colaba Transit Camp, Bombay and he agreed to take on and look after both, Kisti as Bar Waiter and Batti Wallah as Batti Wallah and kitchen hand. Kisti was amazed and gratified to learn that he might receive tips. I do hope they thrived in their new surroundings. I expect they did. Both were resilient and enterprising.

Advice to present-day tourists in Mumbai who might be enticed to take a tour to Elephanta is don't fail to miss it. Not see it, miss it. In my day there was nothing to see in Elephanta except a few dank, smelly caves. On my arrival in January 1944 I met Alan Williams, a young infantry subaltern who, before the war, had been a trainee manager at the Imperial hotel, Torquay. Like me, had no idea what he was supposed to be doing in Elephanta. Enquiries revealed that we were the advance party of the crazy enterprise of Button Scheme, an invasion of Burma across the Bay of Bengal

Alan Williams

and removal or obliteration of the Japs holed up in a redoubt North of Rangoon. Burma was a protectorate of Britain in exchange for certain trading rights and other favours. The Burmese saw it as the job of our army and navy to rid them of invaders and squatters, which the Japs undoubtedly were. It was believed that the cheapest and most effective way of achieving this would be by a seaborne invasion on Burma's west coast. We had no ALC's (assault landing craft.) They had all been wrecked or were beyond repair after D Day.

In those days the Army was not put off by such small details. ALC's could be replaced by dhows, traditional Arab trading craft with a single sail. A team of men were despatched to the Trucial States, small independent protectorates of Britain's in the Persian Gulf (Kuwait, Qatar, Dubai etc.) to buy suitable craft. £400 was the maximum we would pay for the purchase of a craft capable of carrying a half-ton truck. Others were to be rented or chartered complete with crews. These ships had been, and were, arriving at Elephanta daily. Our first job was to test the seaworthiness of the craft. This was achieved by getting twenty men to stand on the gunwales and jump up and down in unison and see if it sank. If it did it was no good. If it still floated it was OK. An American outboard motor was fitted to the rear of each craft to assist the sail. All this work was supervised by Alan Williams. My job was to supervise the waterproofing of the various vehicles which were to be loaded on the dhows. This involved extending the exhaust pipes and air intakes to above the water line, and waterproofing sparking plugs and distributor heads with caps. It was reckoned that the vehicles would be able to proceed in two feet of water thus protected. All very basic and makeshift but tests showed that it worked reasonably well. We already knew that the landing site in Burma was to be in shallow water with a firm base of sand. R.E.M.E experts on loan to us, advised on the waterproofing.

All seemed to be going well when our labours were interrupted by a brass-hat inspection to see how we were getting on. The senior officer in charge of this inspection, a Lieutenant General, immediately objected that two army officers were being employed on what was quite clearly, to him, naval work. He said that we must be replaced by two suitably qualified naval officers at once. It was pointed out to him that Alan and I had been specially trained in this work and naval men would not know the ropes. "In that case," said the brass-hat, "have them transferred to the RN (Royal Navy) and that should keep everybody happy." We were to attend the Royal Naval headquarters in Bombay to have this effected. This is an example of the barmy behaviour of some senior Service people in those halcyon days approaching the end of the war. I immediately objected to such a transfer as it might interfere with my Japanese Campaign pay and comfortable style of life. Alan thought this was a hopeless attitude. In the navy, he said, there was a much smarter uniform which might help even me to pull the chicks in.

On arrival at the RN headquarters, which fortunately happened to be on a race day, we were told that before pursuing the matter we needed naval medical checks. Alan sailed through his. I was turned down flat on the grounds of inadequate eyesight. After a nice afternoon at the races, followed by a celebration dinner at the Turf Club, same as the one in Poona, we both made our ways back to Elephanta to report the bad news. Never mind was the attitude, Just carry on with your jobs as army officers and nobody will know the difference.

The convoy was to proceed down the west coast of India and stop at Cochin for water and supplies. Then round the southern tip of India and across the Bay of Bengal, to a point on the coast of Burma, about 30 mile north of Rangoon. Eventually it was time to set off. Each boat carried a 15-cwt pick-up truck, twenty men and their supplies and armaments, including mortars, grenades and carbine rifles. There was no radio contact with the flotilla leader or any other of the boats. Such signalling that was required was by semaphore, which nobody understood and was soon superseded by shouting. One of the men had a small radio set which he guarded jealously and would not let anybody else near. It was a Decca and operated by lifting the lid. The owner would perform this operation at 6 o'clock GMT each evening just in time to squat round it and hear the chimes of Big Ben on the BBC World Service and the brief headlines of the news. Then the lid would be slammed down and the set shut off to save the battery. We were delighted to find that the local bazaar had plenty of these nine-volt batteries for sale. We also soon learned, having parted with our money, that all were duds, totally exhausted, flat and useless.

On January 10, 1944 we set sail. There was little for the men to do except sun bathe, play cards and fish. For a few days it was quite pleasant but inevitably started to bore. Only three days later we had the lid of the radio open for a few seconds to hear this announcement, "This is the national programme from London. Here is the World News read by Alvar Liddel. A giant bomb of unparalleled size and destructive power has been dropped by the United States Air Force onto the city of Hiroshima in Japan, causing havoc over a wide area of the city and its surroundings. It said that thousands of buildings have been raised to the ground and vast numbers of men, women and children killed or wounded. The Japanese emperor has already sued for peace. All hostilities in the SEAC area of war are to cease by 9am tomorrow." With that, the battery finally petered out and we could hear no more. We had heard enough. At last the war was over! We could all go home! Oh no, we couldn't. A message delivered in a rowing boat from the flotilla leader, who was in short wave radio contact with Delhi Headquarters, told us that there was no official news yet about the end of the war and we would carry on across the ocean until there was. Eventually, a day later, it came through and that really was the end of Button scheme!

Early in the war in India I began to worry about earning a living after the war I had no marketable qualification for anything. I was struck by an advertisement in Tit Bits, or it could have been Answers, for an organisation called The Bennett College in Sheffield, which offered a correspondence course in journalism, price 19 guineas, on completion of which, with no previous experience, one could become a highly paid sports reporter, film reviewer, book critic or foreign correspondent. Any of those would have done. I still had a little money in my English bank account so off went my 19gns. The weekly parts followed me all round India and Burma, via a field post office, with amazing regularity thanks to the excellence of the local and Army postal services. In some way it kept me in touch with normality. Mr Bennett did not teach his pupils how to write English. They were supposed to have learned that at school. He did teach the mechanics of journalism, i.e. how to present copy and how a sub-editor should improve and correct it. I found it useful, interesting and enjoyable. After the war it helped me find a job as a sports reporter, though not, regrettably, a highly paid one.

I was brought up in Chester, a lovely town with a great horse-racing tradition. Every year there was a three day meeting which included the Chester Cup, a big race always run on the first Wednesday of May. This was my introduction to the unjustness of life. It could easily have been on the Tuesday, or the Thursday, but no. It had to be Wednesday, the day I was to be back at boarding school after the Easter holidays. I pleaded with my father to write to say it would be wise if I delayed my return until the Friday because I had a temporary but seriously infectious chill. It would not be wished that every boy in the school and all the masters would be brought down by it. My father was totally uncooperative. Usually I could easily get round my mother if I refrained from whingeing and offered something in return. I promised to work extra hard all next term and do all the washing up next holidays at the special rate of sixpence for dinner and less for all other meals. This was grudgingly accepted and I dictated a suitable letter to the headmaster which was, I recall, something of a masterpiece.

Every morning during race week I would be at the entrance of the Grosvenor, Chester's and Cheshire's leading hotel. The doorman was Mr Simkins, always attired in a smart grey military greatcoat and cockaded top hat. His job was to deny entrance to the hotel via the revolving front door to anybody who looked unsuitable, which would be anybody he did not recognise. He was always very kind to me and gave me a non-stop commentary about all the important arrivals. My boyhood heroes were not football players, racing car drivers or film stars but famous racing men like Gordon Richards, the champion jockey, Tommy Weston, Lord Glanely, and the top owners and trainers. Mr Simkins was on friendly terms with all of them and would describe them to me with non-stop thumb-nail sketches. I was entranced. One year an arrival in a black Daimler saloon car was a youngish-looking man in a smart double-breasted suit flapping open to reveal an equally smart and unusual double-breasted waistcoat. Flowing behind him as he stepped out of a rear car door, opened by Mr Simkins and as though on a kite string, was a mackintosh, a brief case and binoculars. He bent down to say something in Mr Simkins's ear and as he did so pressed something into his gloved hand. By standing on tip-toe I could just see that it was a ten shilling note. Good God, I thought. Ten bob, just for opening a car door. Can you believe it!

Who, I said in wonder to Mr Simkins, was that? "That gentleman said Mr Simkins, "was Mr. Vernon Morgan, Reuters' racing correspondent and a very important man." I immediately resolved to have Mr Morgan's job when grew up or, if not, one very much like it.

"He's just given me Song'O Saxpence in the first," went on Mr Simkins. "Have a fiver on it, he said. Must be a real good thing". Within seconds this information had percolated every nook and cranny of the Grosvenor Hotel, from the boot blacks in the basement to the chambermaids in the attics and the tip had been elaborated from being a "good thing" into a certainty which would win by ten lengths.(It lost.)

I can now reveal, exclusively to those who are interested, that a Mr Vernon Morgan, of Reuter's, does not exist. Never did exit and probably never will exist. He was the brain child of Fred Harrison, erstwhile racing editor of the Press Association. The editor of Reuter's, which was partially owned by the P.A, had asked Fred to produce regular snippets of racing gossip of general interest, culled from the mountains of material produced by P.A. Racing every day for Reuter's to circulate world-wide and, of course to pay for. Nobody did anything for nothing. (Note: Gossip",in the world of P.A., is not what it means to civilians (non-journalists). The P.A meaning was news items which were short, self-contained, and interesting. In P.A., unlike the rest of the newspaper world, truth was sacrosanct because P.A. dealt only in facts. If one wanted to write something which was not true, it had to be under the umbrella of another branch of P.A., 'P.A. Reuter Features

Ltd'. Thus sheltered, one could write the most appalling lies if the occasion warranted. A stipulation was that however unimportant, each of these 'fillers' was to be headed by the Vernon Morgan by-line. This was not to make it look more important but for ease of identification when Fred sent the bills out. Although PA partly owned Reuter's, the two were autonomous in profit and copy sharing. Neither side would give the other a paragraph if it were not paid for.

Sporting Gossip was a particularly popular feature among newspaper "stone men", one of whom was Wilson Stevens, of The Star, a rag evening tabloid, now regrettably defunct, aimed at a readership whose individual vocabularies did not exceed four hundred words. (Other words could be used only with the written permission of the news editor.) Wilson was a popular Fleet Street character whose job it was to make up pages of his paper from the array of "slugs", or chunks of type-face, of varying lengths (commonly lines of about five to ten words which had been spewed out by the Linotype machine awaiting manual assembly. Often there were too many, or too few, to produce a symmetrical whole. If too few, Vernon's "fillers" were produced from his waistcoat pockets. He showed me a selection, including, proudly, his favourite, which, he said, he had so far used seven times that year, including that very morning, at the foot of an innocuous story at the foot of page 2 without anybody noticing. It read: "A bumper raspberry crop is expected in Kent this year." It was his sheer bad luck that the main front page main lead story of the first (of the eight editions which would appear that day, beneath 72-point screamer banner headlines, the largest which would fit on the page, read: FREAK HAIL STORMS BATTER KENT FRUIT FARMS. RASPBERRY CROPS RUINED, SAY GROWERS. It was not a strong story but, in a slow day for news, nothing of more interest or importance had emerged during press hours so it remained undisturbed throughout the eight editions. In spite of the phrenetic nature of his work Wilson held court each morning in the front bar of The Bell where he regaled his many fans with tales of Fleet Street lore. He would often remain at this post for as long as the pints kept flowing or closing time.

Mr Morgan was a gentleman of eclectic tastes. Apart from being an expert on horse-racing he was a keen theatre-goer and was often seen at first nights at the opera, important concerts and major sporting venues like Wimbledon. He had two personal letterheads, one of which contained the information that he was a member of the National Union of Journalists which he would use only for addressees who were known to be left wing, like anybody in the National Theatre. Fred had instructed him that when writing to request free tickets one should always work in the expression "with your customary courtesy" He said it was a magic phrase, never known to fail.

I had been dismayed to learn that P.A. salaries were on a very low level. All sub-editors, like me, were on the same union minimum of 12guineas a week. Dustmen in Wandsworth, were on exactly the same miserable stipend but Wandsworth Council, unlike P.A., was in the unremitting stranglehold of the most pitiless, richest and greediest union in the country. The wretched BBC news subs had to support their wives and mistresses on 8 gns. a week). I cheered up a bit when the senior P.A. Racing Reporter, who was also a well-known writer and broadcaster, told me had never spent a penny of his salary in all the years he had been with PA. He paid his rent and everything else entirely out of surpluses from expenses.

I soon started to love Fleet Street. There was a delightful tradition there that one must go out of one's way to be kind, helpful and supportive to newcomers. Everybody was. After a few days I was offered some overtime reporting at an evening speedway meeting at Wembley Stadium (5guineas). P.A. did not usually cover speedway but the Daily Mail, for some reason, had requested a "special" on this particular event and who were we to turn business away? In the Press Box there was a table laden with food and liquor. About six other press men were there. After a cordial exchange of introductions I explained that I knew nothing about speedway and did not even know how to score. "Don't worry about that," they said. "Just sit down and have a nice time and we'll do it for you. Daily Mail, you said? 300 words should do. Leave it to us." I phoned their story through later and heard no more about it. No news is good news in Fleet Street so this seemed a good start to my new and unexpected career as a speedway reporter.

MULE FACT FILE

A Mule is a cross between a male donkey and female horse.

The reverse, from a male horse and a female donkey is a hinny, is generally useless as a draft, pack, or saddle animal. Mules have a fast but shallow trot and do not lift their legs very high so the rider cannot easily rise in the stirrups, making for an uncomfortable ride.

All Mules are sterile and cannot reproduce. They are great weight carriers and can carry much more than horses of similar size.

Mules have a reputation of being stubborn. This is unjustified. They may seem lazy but they are often highly intelligent. They think there is no point in being asked to jump an obstacle if they can walk round it. They do not take kindly to being asked to perform any task which they consider beyond them.

Chindit Mules were all from an exceptional strain, bred and raised in South Africa. South Africans have a tradition of breeding fine pack mules. Their forefathers, the voortrekkers, could not have colonised the Transvaal without them.

Jim Hough

The bearded Chindit in this picture, a muleteer, is carrying a shoulder-slung Lee Enfield 303 rifle, widely used in the British Army since the start of the Boer War 1903). The magazine carried only five rounds plus one in the breach) It was cumbersome and heavy, although highly successful as a target rifle. It is still widely used at Bisley to this day. It was almost useless as the snap shooting weapon which is required in jungle warfare. The Japs were worse off. Their infantry soldiers carried a weapon even more unsuitable and heavier, bolt-action Mauser type Arisaka first used in 1905. A senior Japanese commander in the field, Ogawa Masatsugu, was quoted after the war as saying that the weapon was "useless and he felt insulted that he was expected to take on British Chindit troops with their vastly superior American equipment and arms. Perhaps this was the reason why Japanese casualties in the period 1943-45 were 13 times heavier than those of British and Empire forces. Note that in the picture above the muleteer is following, rather than leading, the mule. The mule knew perfectly well where he was going. He was following the mule in front. This is what he had been trained to do. Whole columns of mules proceeded like this across Burma, up and down mountain ranges in and out of rivers. The terrain shown is typical of much that we had to travel throughout the campaign, both in training and on serious business. It was seldom possible to travel more than 10 miles in a day.

Mules fording the river Chindwin at a point south of Imphal.

There would be a halt every hour for 10 minutes. In this time the men would make a fire and brew the tea. A British soldier cannot travel far without his tea. They were experts in lighting a fire made from damp kindling and boiling the water within 10 minutes. Small quantities of bone dry kindling were kept in an oilskin tobacco pouch carried on various parts of their persons to keep it dry.

When alight it was a hands-and-knees job with gentle blowing to start it then rising in a steady crescendo until the flame was safely set. The entire operation was an art form. Smoke had to be kept to a bare minimum to avoid attention from Nips. Where the river was deep enough the mules swam across. Mules, unlike horses, are unwilling swimmers. They seemed to have a death wish and would not hold their nostrils above the water. Therefore, for our last and largest crossing, involving all the remaining mules they were towed across by inflated rubber dinghies propelled by outboard motors. Both had been delivered by air drop. Heads were held high above water level by rope or leather head collars. The operation took two days. At the end of it the mules had a hot bran mash. We had a K-ration snack and, for an extra special treat, in the evening, a Vera Lynn concert! We sat around on the ground and each officer was given a bottle of Cyprus gin (even worse than Indian gin), to be shared with two other officers, and each man three bottles of beer. Few of us had had an alcoholic drink for up to three months. Behaviour was, at best, imperfect but Vera was a real sport. What a truly great lady. Later, of course, she became a Dame and deservedly so.

The mules had usually been fed only once a day, at the end of the day's march. First they were watered, if possible by running water, as mules are very fussy about what they drink. We were entirely reliant on air drops for fodder, of which there was never enough. There was little wild forage. Grass did not exist anywhere except in small clumps of weeds. Bamboo shoots were usually available, but the mules did not greatly care for them. This is just as well because bamboo is of very low calorific value. At the end of an average day's march the muleteer would spend at least an hour of his spare time searching for other forage for his mule. Almost all the muleteers became very attached to their animals and spent much time grooming and tending to their many minor cuts, scratches harness sores and other injuries. When the men had time to attend to themselves, if not on guard duty, they would sit down and remove their boots, often a very painful process because of soreness and blisters, and make a start on removing leeches. If one had walked through stagnant water they would always be there, embedded in flesh in their dozens or, as I have known to my personal discomfort, hundreds. It was impossible to escape these repulsive, blood-sucking creatures. They could get through anything, even the lace-holes of boots. It was a waste of time chopping their heads or tails off because they immediately grew another and scampered off quite happily scattering one's blood around. A preferred solution was to incinerate them with a lighted Victory "V" cigarette, and then not always successfully because that dreadful fag would expire before the job was done. Life on a Chindit column could be very trying.

November 3, 2008,

Dear Dame Vera,

We met in Burma in early 1944, not far from Imphal. You had called on a Chindit column of which I was a member and gave us one of your memorable concerts. It was a great occasion and, for you, a personal triumph. Everybody was in high spirits because the Japs were being soundly trounced for the first time and it seemed that the war on our front might soon be over. After an alfresco dinner the officers were lined up to be introduced to you.

In the course of our quite short conversation you were informed that I was an animal officer, in charge of 400 mules. I might have told you that only the previous day I had been involved in swimming and wading many of them across the river Chindwin. You told me that you had been reading about these remarkable animals and how it would have been impossible to win the war without them. You asked me what would happen when we had no further use for them. I had to tell you that it had already been decided that they would be painlessly put down. We would not give them to the native Burmese as we had all witnessed the disregard and cruelty with which domestic animals were treated in Burma. No way would we allow our mules to suffer their fate.

You said that you were appalled to hear this and what a dreadful way to repay these noble animals after their devoted and invaluable service. You are an animal lover and had a good deal to say on the subject.

There was, just behind you, a man with red and white flashes of WAR CORRESPONDENT on his shoulders, the first I had seen in four years service in the SEAC area. I had noticed his total disinterest in your concert but he was now pointedly and rudely listening to every word of our conversation and writing it down.

I believe he was from the Daily Mirror. I know, Dame Vera, that one of your greatest admirers was Winston Churchill. He admired you not only for your talents as a singer and entertainer but also for your great work in upholding public morale, particularly that of the troops. It would not be stretching the bounds of imagination too far to guess that before leaving on your hazardous adventures abroad with the concert party organisers, ENSA, (he would have invited you to contact him direct should you encounter some unfortunate circumstance which you could not deal with yourself. He would have given you his private telephone number on which he was available round the clock as he almost never slept).

Such a circumstance might have been the plight of our mules and it is my belief that you managed to phone Winnie and plead with him to stop this monstrous injustice. Normally it would have been impossible for you or anybody else to telephone London from the depth of a Burmese jungle. You could do it because you were not just Vera Lynn; you were also the Force's Sweetheart. You could have done anything.

As a further demonstration of my imagination I can see Winston propped up in bed next day in front of four pillows (I have read that he never rose before 11am right through the war) and reading the Daily Mirror. He loathed and detested that newspaper (and sued them once) but always read it before The Times. He saw that it had led with its Vera and the Mules story on the front page, deeming it more important than the horror stories which were emerging from Germany about the underground bunkers and the haggard displaced persons who were only just daring to rise to the surface and show themselves.

Later that morning I was attending a meeting of top SEAC officials in a railway carriage. Bill Slim, the Field Marshal, Commander of the 14th Army,was one of the dignitaries present. There was also Major General Arthur Snelling, Chief of the Indian Army, Commander Michael Snelling of the Royal Navy, his son and others, including a senior RAF officer. I was taking the minutes. A messenger entered, came right up to me and handed me an Army telegram form, written in pencil and addressed: Animal Officer, Queen's Royal, 14th Army and our numeric field Post Office number. It was from The Cabinet Office, London SW1. The message was brief and unequivocal. DO NOT SHOOT MULES. CHURCHILL.

Vera, neither I nor anybody else, except the Mirror, who presumably thought it made more dramatic copy, had suggested that the mules were to be shot, and neither, at this time, to make it quite clear, were they shot. or painlessly otherwise. I believe it was you who saved their lives.

I should explain why, as the lowly Animal Officer, I was taking the minutes at such an important meeting. In those days most officers were frequently moved around and transferred to various other units of the service and they were frequently called upon to perform duties well beyond their normal experience. They had to carry with them a form, which today would be known as a CV, carrying details of their previous experience, courses attended and roles performed. The last entry was "Civilian Occupation". I had found that putting down "Student" or "Estate Agent's Clerk" was getting me nowhere. A more grandiose occupation might help. I once tried "Biscuit Manufacturer". A mistake, as I was soon in immediate danger of being transferred to the Catering Corps, to a Chindit the ultimate disgrace. I escaped this just in time and substituted "Newspaper Reporter" on my CV. I considered this justified as the Chester Chronicle had printed a short piece of mine, headed "From one of the Lads Overseas" without a credit or, indeed, payment.

*   *   *

Preparatory to the aforesaid meeting at the railway carriage, which had been stripped of its doors, carriage partitions and most of its seats, to make more room, a Major from General Staff, quite a bigwig, came up to me and told me I was to take the minutes of the meeting. I immediately protested that I was totally unqualified for such a task.

"Ridiculous," he said, clutching my CV. "It says here you were a Newspaper Reporter."

"Maybe," I replied, "but my shorthand is shockingly rusty." I was told not to argue the toss and just get on with it.

The President of the meeting, a Lieutenant General, was standing on a chair in a corner of the carriage. He said there was no room for me to sit and I must squat on the floor by his feet. The meeting had been called to discuss the arrangements and logistics for dispersal of troops, equipment and my mules when hostilities finally seized, which would be any day now. Shortly after the meeting started I started to feel slightly light-headed. About a hundred men were in the carriage, standing and all smoking, as men did in those days. Little fresh air could circulate and the atmosphere was dreadful. My condition worsened because of the surfeit of Cyprus gin consumed the night before. I slipped off into a dead faint on the floor. I slowly came to and was discovered, prostrate, at the end of the meeting. The carriage was empty. Everybody had gone. I had not written a word of the minutes. Amazingly, I did not receive the expected rockets and nobody said a word about it. Somebody else wrote up the minutes from memory.

In view of Churchill's telegram, I was informed that the mules were to go to a Remount Depot in Bangalore. A Remount Depot was a home for Army horses. In those days all British officers in India were entitled to have a "charger". On payment of 100 rupees (£7.50p) they could chose from a large selection of polo ponies, racehorses, show jumpers, and other good mounts, usually all thoroughbreds, which were readily available from a remount depot, of which there were many dotted around India. When the horse was no longer required (e.g. lame) it could be returned and the hundred rupees refunded.

The railway authorities provided an extraordinary train for the purpose of moving the mules. There were about 14 cattle trucks, each partitioned each to take 10 animals. There was a passenger coach to take the team of muleteers and another, for me, which had previously been the property of a Maharajah and much space was taken up with his personal requirements such as a kitchen, bathroom, thunder box WC, servants' and guest room. His furniture, according to an inventory on the wall, included, surprisingly, an escritoire in the Louis XIV style. Also listed was a chaise longue, a mahogany dining table, six dining chairs, two carvers, a canteen of cutlery and a china cabinet with a complete Royal Doulton dinner service (some missing) and a posted bed with drapes and linen cabinet.

There were no loading ramps anywhere near our camp. The mules had to be walked to a watering halt, about 8 miles away, where there was a walk-up raised platform suitable for loading them. This was an enormously difficult task. We had to cram in the animals very close together, not only to save space but to prevent them kicking and injuring each other. I do not usually excel at tasks involving manual labour but I do claim a certain expertise when it comes to loading mules onto trains. The correct procedure is not unlike that of loading racehorses into starting stalls. A mule or a racehorse thinks he is boss on such occasions and needs to be taught otherwise. We have all witnessed pathetically puerile attempts of professional handlers on television trying to load racehorses, often highly-strung and frightened, into starting stalls. It is sometimes an object lesson in how not to do it. The groom should lead the horse up to the stall on a leading rein, then pause at the open door so that the horse can see there is no nasty bogey man or other horror lurking about inside waiting to pounce. There is not, so both enter, the horse looking ahead and the groom at his side. What happens next is the ultimate in stupidity. The groom turns to the horse, faces it and then the camera in case his mum is watching. A horse does not like being looked at, especially stared at. It thinks it is being "taken on", so it plants all four feet and refuses to budge another inch. In any staring match between a human and a horse there would be only one loser and it would not be a quadruped. The groom should do what he is paid to do, that is to walk on into the stall beside the horse, and forget about his tiresome old mother. The horse will walk in with him. Guaranteed.

When installed, the mule has to be kept quiet while his neighbour is fed, watered or groomed (for removal of parasites). This is best effected by one of his legs being raised off the ground. A mule likes to pretend that he cannot stand on three legs. He can, but cannot do anything else at the same time. Like a small child, he needs his nose and eyes wiped clean regularly. This is best effected by a square of knitted cotton called a sponge cloth supplied by the Army for the purpose and in reality a dishcloth The mule would often mistake it for a pre-luncheon appetiser. His long tongue would snake out; wrap itself round the cloth which would in a flash disappear down his gullet. After a period it reappeared at his other end. I was amazed to see that it was apparently only slightly damaged by mastication and semi-digestion. When we had amassed a collection I found they could be restored to near-enough original condition by application of a hose pipe in a large tub. Knowing of the Army's obsession with parsimony, I prepared a memo on the phenomenon and submitted to the appropriate authorities in the hope that it might one day help towards promotion and salary increase, sorely needed. To date I have heard nothing.

Progress on the train was boringly slow, seldom more than10mph. Initially we were on a single track and were frequently shunted on to a sideline to let other traffic pass. After three days we found ourselves rumbling across Hardinge's Bridge. The guns were still there but covered in heavy tarpaulins which would cause the barrels to sweat and rust. I had never been officially relieved of my post at the Bridge and had half a mind to halt the train and call for an inspection. Loud cries of dissent, mutinous if taken seriously, dissuaded me. We fed the mules once a day, at dusk. Watering was more of problem. They needed water more often and such was their desperation for it that they would knock the galvanized pail over and waste the water. More than once they damaged their mouths on the rim, where it meets the handle. We had a few canvas buckets which held less water but were safer so we managed with those. We could have indented for more but that would have given the supply supremo apoplexy so we managed with those we had. At Pabna station, which was a junction we knew from our ice run, we stopped to receive rations delivered by the unit who had taken over at The Bridge. There were no "K" rations but plenty of good quality fresh beef packed in ice and ample bread and vegetables. We had no trained army cooks with us. Mostly ours had only a slight notion of what they were doing but the general standard was not bad and certainly edible. Cooks were detailed for the job day by day along with spud and veg. bashers. This was not unusual. Some were better than others. In the Army soldiers have to do a bit of everything. All cooking had to be performed on the usual Army upright cylindrical charcoal stove with a lift-off lid for rapid boiling. Dinner, the mid-day meal, was prepared by boiling a Dixie about one-third full of water and then flinging in some fairly large chunks of beef, potatoes of same size and perhaps carrots or leeks if available. Then the lid was replaced, to cut down the heat, and the rest was simplicity itself. It went on cooking itself until it tasted ready Salt and pepper, and perhaps a whole pot of Marmite, and/or or a generous slug of tomato ketchup, were added at the whim of the chef.

We had two 100-gals. water tanks on the train for drinking, cooking, ablutions, laundry, mule watering and mucking out Early next morning, on arrival at Nagpur, another large junction, in the very dead centre of India, we were routed to a siding for tank checking and refills. While halted a uniformed railway employee was parading the platform shouting

("Chota hazri! Chota hazri!

That meant breakfast. I had already searched the station platform for a kitchen, a dining room or a shop but there was none. I asked the man where was the chota hazri?" On the train Sahib, he said.

The coolest seat on the train was in an open doorway.

"We bring it you, on a tray. Very very, very nice. Everybody like. Best chota hazri in India! He showed us the price list.

Three eggs any style, bacon, sausage, tomato and mushrooms with coffee or tea and toast, butter and jam four chips or six bob. The bargain of all time! Any style eggs included, we were assured, sunny side up, so I, Sgt. Haynes and four of the unmarried men on duty in my carriage immediately stumped up. No married men. They could not possibly afford it. Because of the miserably small allowances the Army paid their wives, barely above subsistence level, which was a national disgrace, the married men usually sent the whole of their pay, including pocket money, home sometimes not even retaining pocket and fag money for cigarettes. On occasions like this it was the custom for all unmarried men including officers, to have a whip round so that nobody went without.

The "Quit India" campaign, orchestrated by the Congress Party, under Pandit Nehru, was now gathering momentum.

While the breakfast order was being administered we had all noticed a small group of commuters waiting on the platform presumably, for a train. They had seen soldiers on our train and had set up a chant for their benefit. QUIT INDIA", they sang. "QUIT, QUIT, QUIT! This was a bit much for our lads.

"Quit India? You daft pillocks! We'd go tomorrow if we could!

QUIT INDIA! QUIT INDIA! Resumed the chorus. "QUIT, QUIT, QUIT!

"BOLLOCKS!" was the shouted reply. WHO DO YOU THINK WOULD RUN THIS CRUMMY COUNTRY IF WE DID?" They added.

"SANTA CLAUS? FRED KARNO? SANDY POWELL? JANE MANSFIELD?

DON'T TALK CRAP!!

One of our number suggested that this line of conversation might prejudice production of our chota hazri which had not yet appeared and might not appear at all if it continued. Our side of the barracking ceased at once.

The engine driver gave a toot of his whistle, a signal for All Aboard and still no breakfast! The conductor gave a preliminary wave of his green flag. The drive wheels gave a couple of practice turns, skidding on the rails with a whoosh of steam. The urgency of the situation was now desperate. A final appeal must be made to the Quit India mob. "Go and get our breakfast you skrimshanking bastards! The lads shrieked. "Either that, or get our money back"

It was too late. The drive wheels now had a grip on the rails and we were slowly gathering speed. Bloody Indians. No hope now. We always knew that, deep down, the whole nation was dishonest. Crooked lot of sods. We sank back on the green leatherette banquette seat and counted our losses.

There was a tapping noise on the window opposite. There was a dark face there with brilliantly white flashing magnesium sparklers in his mouth, only they weren't sparklers. They were teeth, inside a wide, smiling mouth. "Chota Hazri, Sahib! said the mouth. As the train rolled along I could see that he was holding on by his left hand clutching an outside brass door handle. On the finger tips of his other hand he was balancing a laden tea tray in the manner of an effete Savoy tea-time tea waiter. "Chota hazri, Sahib", he said, "Sorry a little bit late! We opened the window and saw five other waiters, queuing up in similarly perilous fashion. Five other laden trays, one by one, were passed in to us. The food had been kept warm by aluminium plate covers secured in place by rubber bands. We had the best breakfasts in India that day.

On leaving Nagpur the train turned left and entered the searing dustbowl of the Deccan plain, towards Hyderabad, a huge district and town, presided over one of the richest men in the world, the Nizam. I had read that one of his predecessors spent most of his life sitting on his gilded throne all day. That was all he did. Or so it was said. Surely there must have been more to it. At his feet was a handmaiden who was paid a large sum of money to stroke one of his feet all day. She only did that until the day the Nizam died, by which time she was a very rich handmaiden. To make life even better for her, she herself was said to be a foot fetishist. She had stashed away more dough during her lifetime than the combined fortunes of the world's two previously richest women, Helen Roebeling, who owned the Brooklyn Bridge, and Barbara Hutton, the Woolworth heiress.

We had heard a radio announcement on All-India radio that a pre-monsoon heat wave had descended on the Deccan Plain. The temperature shot up to 100 deg. Fahrenheit (about 40 Centigrade) almost off the scale and was bearable only if the windows and both carriage doors were left wide open.

From then on the line went down hill all the way to Bangalore. The train gently free-wheeled into a siding. All of us, including the mules, had a good drink, a good meal and a good rest.

THE TROOPSHIPS

In 1942 I had travelled from Liverpool to Durban on the P&O SS.Ormonde (3 weeks), and thence to Bombay on Dunera (ten days), a small ship owned by a line with the long-winded title of British India and Oriental Steam Navigation Co. Dunera had been launched only in1940 and this was its maiden voyage. At that time there was an extreme shortage of shipping. Later it was sold, refitted and renamed Uganda and became a well known as a popular cruise ship for school children.

En route for Bombay seven young officers were packed into a cabin for four, so four slept on bunks and three on the floor. We changed round in turns. This was uncomfortable but the men were much worse off. They slept in airless holds with the hatches off for ventilation. Many preferred the open deck in all weathers. There were 2000 on our ship. It was built to take 300. Men took it in turns to wash and eat. All cabins, baths, lounges, restaurants and bars were for officers only. All drinks were sixpence and there was no shortage. This is an extreme example of the huge gulf in living standards between officers and men in the army, particularly on troopships, at that time. It was widely accepted as normal by officers and men.

On the Bombay-Liverpool run we were on the much larger Monarch of Bermuda. There was an enormous first class lounge which stretched the entire width and most of the length of the ship. All upholstery was in brown hide which struck me as being unnecessarily sombre. Food was excellent. On our first day on I was delighted to see plump Manx kippers on the breakfast table, the first I had seen in seven years.

The Captain told me that he would employ only Lascars (Indian Orientals) as crew. He said that in his long experience they made the best seamen, cooks, air gunners and hotel staff. (Yes, air-gunners. Our Merchant Navy was not provided with air defence. It was up to them to provide their own, with useless Lewis Guns from the Boer War).

The Suez Canal was jammed with sunk or partially sunken bombed ships. The Egyptians were now in charge and it was widely prophesied that they would make a mess of organizing it. I do not know why people should have thought this because the Egyptians did most of the work when the Brits were running the show. The Egyptians were now working throughout the days and by floodlight throughout the nights aided by the Royal Navy clearing the mess away. They were slowly succeeding.

The only entertainment was a non-stop game of Bingo, broadcast on the ship's tannoys. There were almost no seats so men sprawled about where they could, some half way up the main mast. Cost was 2/6d a game. To save time collecting the money they were sold in minimum lots of eight (£1) and some groups of men formed syndicates to cut down the cost. Stakes from un-won games were added to a rollover jackpot which might reach £500, a sum which, added to a forthcoming gratuity, might be enough for a down payment on a news-tob-conf* with flat above, the pinnacle of an average soldier's ambition.

*News, tobacco and confectionary shop.

Excitement mounted as we cruised past Gibraltar. Then it was full steam ahead (18knots) for the last roll-over jackpot, Liverpool and home!

We had hoped to be greeted at the Docks by union jacks and pretty girls blowing kisses at us but the quayside was empty and deserted. There was a solitary and desultory train. We entrained, as the Army would say. Next stop was Gravesend, home of my Regiment, the Queen's Royal, for demobilisation formalities and collection of gratuities. In the evening I sat down and composed a careful letter to Sir Henry Martin, Editor-in Chief of the Press Association, as from my home address in Chester. I said that I had it in mind to become his Racing Correspondent, though possibly not in those exact words. He replied most charmingly, saying how kind it was of me to write and explained that he already had forty such correspondents but all was not lost because if they all moved up a bit perhaps room could be found for me. I knew I would like Sir Henry. I wrote back thanking him and confirmed the date he suggested, about a week ahead. Next day it was another long train journey to Staveley, Derbyshire and its demob centre. We were to select a kit of civilian clothes there. The only suits left were of brown glencheck. There was another man there grumbling about these. I was delighted to see that it was Neil Heap, whom I had not seen for years, a very old friend, Cheshire Yeoman and Boudoir Boy. It was no coincidence that we met at the Stavely Demob Centre. Demobilisation was strictly in date of birth order and Neil and I were the same age and shared the same birthday. After collecting the rest of our kit (shoes, underwear, felt hat, socks, etc. and a massive number of clothing coupons, which I would never need, I gave some to my sister in Chester who fell on them with whoops of delight. We were given first class railway warrants to go anywhere we liked. We both chose London and checked in at an officers' club in Piccadilly, incredibly cheap, about six shillings a night. Only two nights' residence was permitted because of the high demand. Next day we found our banks and banked our gratuities. Mine was addressed to Lieut. H.J.Hough, whereas I was a Captain. I received £346. With it was a letter from The King thanking me for my loyal and selfless service and saying that I would be permitted to retain my rank, pay, and uniform of lieutenant for six months.

In the evening we saw Oklahoma at Drury Lane. The only seats left were six shillings in the pit. Dreadful mistake. A mile from the stage, inaudible and invisible. Since then I have refused to see any show at Drury Lane unless from the front stalls. Next day we finished some essential shopping and had lunch at The Chicken Inn, London's first fast food restaurant, in Haymarket. We had thigh and chips, 211d. Amongst much merriment between us we read out, aloud, Situations Vacant and Businesses For Sale from the Evening Standard. Some of the latter were obtainable for a price well within that of a Monarch of Bermuda Jackpot Full House. A man who had been sitting a few seats away pushed his plate aside and came round to speak to us.

"Not withstanding the unseemly racket you were making, gentlemen, I could not help overhearing you are looking for work. If either or both would care to come and see me after your lunch I may be able to offer you something." He placed a card before us. It read:

WAKEFIELD FORTUNE AND CO.

INTERNATIONAL SHIPPERS AND FORWARDERS,

Suite 3D,

5TH FLOOR,

34A SHAFTESBURY AVENUE,

LONDON WC1

Neil and I went and saw that it was an otherwise deserted building. Access to the 5th floor was by a very old creaking lift, operated by heaving on a rope. I said I was not going in as I was making no plans until I had seen Sir Henry at PA.

Neil went on alone. In the afternoon I concluded my shopping by buying a scrapbook. I must have been mad. It was a magnificent affair of hand-made vellum and bound in goatskin. It cost the monstrous sum of eight guineas. Back at the Club there was a note for me from Neil saying that he had got the job and been sent to Cologne, Germany, immediately. He would be in touch. After a few postcards from him and a Christmas card from New York we lost contact. I spent the evening pasting up and preparing my beautiful cuttings book to show Sir Henry.

The war was over and I had spent much time at the end of it in Bombay and became friendly with two Anglo Indian brothers, Ivan and Eugene d'Avoines. Together they ran but did not own a daily racing newspaper, The Sporting Times, on the lines of our Racing Post but mostly much better. One of their features was a panoramic picture of every race finish, first ten places. None of that boring dog racing rubbish. Both men had been trained on The Times of India. They were not only proficient journalists but knew all about the production side of newspapers. There could be nowhere in the world better, or cheaper than Bombay to publish a newspaper. Theirs was printed by The Times of India which had first class, modern equipment and they charged The Sporting Times £30000 rupees per 10,000copies, including the newsprint. The cover price was 4 rupees. Add the considerable advertising revenue and you can see a viable business. A full page was 1000 rupees, usually taken by Krishna; Bombay's biggest bookmaker. I seriously considered starting a similar paper. Not in Bombay Perhaps. Kuala Lumpur could have been a better bet with its larger and growing racing community, and greater general prosperity and more promising future. I had not, of course, forgotten South Africa. I prepared two features for The Sporting Times, covering the two centre pages. One was on India's School for Jockeys which had been founded two years before, for homeless boys or ones from very poor families. The idea was to produce Indian apprentice jockeys as almost all jockeys riding on Indian tracks were English, Australian or French. The boys were well fed and clothed, received a basic education in English and arithmetic and were taught horse management and riding. It was hoped that those who could not make it as jockeys would be able to earn a living as stable hands or riding boys. The enterprise was entirely supported by a charity funded by The Royal West Indian Turf Club. In two previous years, at the Kirkee races, after the main events, there had been races for the boys from the school with small cash prizes for the first three who were loudly applauded. The boys were properly dressed with smart white breeches, racing boots, owners' colours and caps. Whips were not allowed and there was no betting. A few trainers attended, looking for emerging talent.

Ivan and Eugene liked the story but declined to pay for it on the grounds that they did not need it. I agreed they could have it for nothing on the condition that they would let me choose my own headlines, by-line and cross heads. It was a good experience for me and I thought it looked satisfactorily professional in my scrap book. On the same conditions I had also prepared another story, with a similarly impressive double-page spread, on the recently discovered science of artificial insemination and how it might affect the valuable industry of thoroughbred bloodstock breeding, now becoming increasingly important in India. It could either boost it or wreck the market depending on one's audience. I told Ivan that the story was largely plagiarised from a small speciality breeding magazine from New Zealand. He was unconcerned. He had never been sued and was sure, he said, never would be as he was too small, had no money and it was too difficult to prove damage.

FLEET STREET

The day I was due to see Sir Henry dawned and I was up bright and early, clad in my brown glenchecks and Oxford lace-up demob shoes, dusted with the bed clothes. Hair was smoothed with a slick of Brylcreem. I made my way to Green Park tube station and thence to Blackfriars (five old pence). I arrived at 85 Fleet Street, PA, Headquarters, still too early so there was time to checkout nearby pubs, cafes and for future use, free parking places (Plenty in Salisbury Square, nearby.) There was an ABC, so in I went for a sit-down and a cup of tea (tuppence h'apenny, a sum so small it cannot be converted into today's currency.) At PA there was a waiting area so I had another free sit down and read the papers. In the next chair was a man who enquired who was I waiting for. I saw no harm in telling him that it was Sir Henry Martin. Did I realise, he wondered, that Sir Henry was a deeply religious man and a renowned world-wide expert on The Holy Bible?

"No," I said. Further, he went on, Sir Henry used his position as a major disseminator of information to promulgate 'The Word' on every possible occasion. If, in the mass of verbiage which left PA every day, his eye fell on a paragraph which displeased him, he was not above re-writing it there and then to include a puff for The Almighty.

I was shown into Sir Henry's office and his welcome could not have been warmer. He gave me a handshake, a pat on the back and helped me off with my £30 Crombie double-breasted overcoat with matching belt and ticket pocket. He carefully folded it and placed it and my hat on the back of a chair.

"Now," he said, settling at his desk. "Let's have a look at this portfolio."

Christ! Shock number one! *Portfolio!* What is the man talking about? Portfolio! I'm a writer, not a bloody artist!

"Something the matter Mr Hough?" asked Sir. Henry.

"You had me slightly worried," I said, "because I associate the word 'portfolio' with paintings or drawings, not writings."

"Could be either or both," said Sir H. "What do you call it?"

"I call it," I said, "but I am probably wrong, a scrapbook or a cuttings book.

"OK We'll settle for scrapbook. Happy now?"

I placed the book before him and he started turning the pages with the speed of a machine gun, hardly looking at any. He reached the middle, with my two page spread of the apprentice jockey school story but gave it no more than a few seconds. I knew, or had been told, that proficient and experienced journalists never read anything. They look at it, of course, but do not read it. They photograph it into their minds then play it back later when they have time to absorb it. At least, that is what I was told. New people like me in The Street (only phonies call it Fleet Street) are considered fair game for having their legs pulled.

Sir Henry read on, with marked disinterest, until he reached my superb double-page spread of the artificial insemination feature. I must say it did look impressive from where I was standing. He pulled his chair further towards him, settled into it more comfortably, started reading and eventually spoke.

"Where," he asked, without looking up, "did you get this stuff?" I'd been rumbled! No point in lying. In any case there was no need. I had a perfect reply.

"It has been an interest of mine for some years," I said.

"How very remarkable," said Sir Henry. Then, "Would you mind if I took it back home so that I can digest it more fully when I have the time? You did a great job there."

"Please," I said, "keep it as long as you like. I am so glad you liked it"

"I'll bring it back tomorrow", he said. Then, "Mr Hough, you said you came here from Chester. How much was the rail fare?" It was twenty-eight shillings but quick as a flash, because I was already falling easily and naturally into the ways of acceptable behaviour in PA, I replied, "Two pounds ten, Sir." There must have been a few extras," he said, "so let's call it three pounds," writing out a petty cash voucher for that amount. "Take this to the Pay Office downstairs and they will refund it to you. You will find it at the end of the News Room, on the right." As I reached the door he called again. "Mr Hough, no need to go all the way downstairs again. Go through that door on the right and you will find a staircase. Go down that and it will lead you straight into the News Room and another thing," he called, "When can you start?" Could you believe it? I was in! The biggest and the best, something I had always wanted to do. Forget all that nonsense about Bombay, Kuala Lumpur, even South Africa. It was going to be London and PA for me. I was totally confident that I could do it, would enjoy it and be good at it. For a start, I did not lack self confidence.

"Would tomorrow be all right?" I asked.

"Marvellous," replied Sir Henry. "Report to Fred Harrison in the Racing room and I'll tell him to expect you." I had closed the door but could hear Sir Henry calling at me again, this time shouting. "Mr Hough", he shouted. "I am so very delighted that you will be joining us." Within a year I would be Assistant Night Editor of the largest and most profitable department in this huge and important firm. I knew I would be good at it.

I found the pay office, signed for my £3 and made for the way out. In the centre of the Newsroom was a small crowd round a tea trolley. I joined them and paused for tea and an iced bun. We were in the very nerve centre of the largest, most influential, widest quoted News Agency in the World.

I stood there savouring the throbbing buzz and excitement of it all, the clattering of the telex and creed machines, non-stop telephones, rushing messengers, even old-fashioned spluttering tape machines. A man came up to me. "What are you doing?" he asked.

"Nothing Sir," I replied.

"Don't call me Sir," he said. "My name is Alf."

"Sorry, Alf" I said.

"You are not paid to do nothing," Alf added and as he spoke he was scribbling on a clip board. He had already written 'Madame Hennesey' and a telephone number. He now added an address, 'Flat D, 27 Rutland gardens, SW1.' He tore off the sheet of paper and gave it me. "She's just arrived in town," he said. "Go and see what she's got."

"About what," I asked.

"How the bloody hell do I know," he said, only he did not say "bloody" but a much naughtier word with sexual implications. It seemed that PA journalists, in the commendable interests of brevity, never found it necessary to complete a sentence. It could be implied by anybody with any sense. "Got" is an awkward word to leave hanging in the air because its real meaning is "begot" or "procreated" and Madame would not have had the opportunity, or, perhaps inclination, in so short a time. I did not, of course, say this as I did not want to upset Alf. The implied missing words were obviously 'to say' and this could only mean an interview. I called Madame's number from a telephone cubicle. A male voice answered.

"My name is James Hough," I said, "and I am a journalist speaking from The Press Association."

"Good morning, Sir," was the polite reply. "This is Madame's butler speaking. Her Ladyship would like me to take any message you may have for her."

"Kindly tell Her Ladyship that I would like to welcome her to London and perhaps have a short interview with her at Rutland Gate this afternoon. If she would be so kind as to agree I need not detain her few more than ten, possibly five, minutes." The reply was that she would be pleased to see me at three o'clock.

I turned up on time and was shown into an ante room where the butler asked if, while waiting, I would like a cup of tea, or perhaps a glass of home made lemonade?

I politely declined both as what I had really hoped for was a nip of her husband's cognac to settle my nerves. I explained to Madame that I had prepared a few questions which she may be kind enough to answer. She was here to buy horses, she said, particularly chasers for marathon races in France and Northern Italy.

While talking I had been tugging at a Pitman's shorthand note book in a hip pocket of my brown glencheck demob trousers. I togged and tugged but it was jammed fast and refused to shift. The book was too big for the pocket. Or the pocket was too small for the book. Whatever the reason I was in trouble because I knew, from a dress rehearsal at the club before leaving, that the only possible way to recover the note book, having arrived at this situation, was to unbutton and remove my trousers. This might have resulted in Madame telephoning the police and ruining the interview. Also it would have effectively scuppered any thin hope there may have been of our brief association blossoming into an altogether more interesting affair involving invitations for lunch or even week-ends at her chateau as Madame, though quite old, was far from unattractive and who could know what opportunities might have presented themselves while her husband was out pruning the vines or whatever. Madame herself came to my rescue.

"Mr Hough,", she said, "Before we start, may I ask you a question?"

"Of course," I replied. "Please do. Anything you wish."

"I do not want to seem rude, or inquisitive, so please do not be offended if that is what I might seem. I only wish to try to help you."

"Madame," I said, "I am sure you could not possibly offend me. Please carry on."

"Right," she replied. "Mr Hough, I really must know where you bought that perfectly frightful suit you are wearing."

"This," I replied, "came from a tailoring firm in England known as the Fifty Shilling Tailors, the Tailors of Taste. It was given to me by a grateful government after seven years in our Fighting Forces." I added that the material was brown glencheck, currently at the peak of male fashion, although that information might not yet have crossed the Channel. Madame said she was pleased to hear this. She added that, if I wished to succeed in my chosen field of employment, which I had told her I was new to, I should change it at once for something more suitable. Gentlemen, for a start, she added, did not wear brown.

My day had been tiring but, I thought, successful and therefore deserved a small celebration in a good restaurant. I decided to walk up The Strand and into the Leicester Square area which was full of places to eat. In St Martin's Lane I saw, on a wall, a huge poster playbill for the variety show at the London Palladium. Top of the bill was Danny Kaye, with letters at least a foot high and I wondered where they got a lead font of that huge size. The answer was that they were not lead. They were wood, which quickly wore out but equally quickly remade on an inexpensive jig. Size of the various names on a playbill was in proportion to their importance. Those who made it only into the very last line merited letters only a few inches high. Beneath that, even smaller was a short description of the act. One hoped this did not give them an inferiority complex. The second last act must have pleased the typesetters because it read TED RAY, only six letters complete. Beneath that was 'fiddlin' & 'foolin'. Ted, we supposed, played the violin, cracked a few jokes and danced a soft shoe shuffle or two.

There was another entry which should have been headed:

DIRECT FROM THE SAVOY THEATRE SCUNTHORPE.

But it was not. There was only 'BETTY DRIVER' and beneath, that, 'Soubrette.'

Good for Betty! She made into a big time show bill even if only onto the last line. A soubrette, should you be wondering, is a theatrical term for a coquettish singing parlour maid with feather duster, black silk stockings and garters.

My immediate intention had been to take Betty for a drink or even dinner but I reflected this might not be a good idea. She could be in the middle of an act, or recovering from an earlier one. She might not remember me. I was just one of the lads hanging around the Savoy stage door and she probably never knew my name. In any case I had only the £3 from PA on me, hardly enough for two to eat and drink. I wisely decided to give Betty a miss this time. Having no immediate cash for emergencies was not normally an inconvenience for a British Army officer. He could walk into any English clearing bank, perhaps penniless, submit a cheque for £3 drawn on his own account, which could be on any bank, not necessarily the one he was in and if in uniform, would immediately be given £3 which would get him back to his unit. There was no danger that the cheque would bounce. Officers were gentlemen. Gentlemen did not give bad cheques. At least, that was the common thinking. Occasionally the system failed and if an officer did issue an unpaid cheque for a substantial amount the man was doomed. Theoretically the punishment was dire and inevitable, that of cashiering, which involved reduction to the ranks, a prison sentence and debarring from any future post in the armed services or in national or local government. This meant that he would be banned from holding a job even as a road sweeper in a local council. In practice, during the war, such punishments were not imposed but officers were still cashiered for fraud involving seriously large cheque offences.

During my last few days in India I was lodged at a transit camp while waiting for the "Monarch" to arrive. I had surrendered my de luxe bungalow. I had the bad luck to be detailed as escort to another officer who was awaiting trial by Court Martial on a charge of larceny.

At the initial hearing he had been discharged, as the Army put it, without prejudice to re-arrest. Regulations in such circumstances were strict. One of them was that the accused officer, who in this case was a captain, had to be guarded and, if necessary, restrained, by an escort of another officer of similar rank. I was the only other captain hanging about the camp apparently doing nothing so guess who was Joe Soap? Me of course. My prisoner proved to be amenable and offered me his parole not to abscond. Had he done so I would have been in it up to here!

It was not an onerous chore as my prisoner proved to be totally submissive. I had to be with him at all times. He was given a bed next to mine and I had to escort him to the lavatory and to the Officers' Mess for meals. As it was he proved an engaging and even amusing character. During our time together he did not have the slightest qualm about the trouble he was in. The circumstances were that he was a temporary Field Cashier seconded from the Royal Army Pay Corps. His job was to travel around India paying officers and men in remote postings that had no access to a pay parade or officers to a bank account. With him was a large bullet-proof steel trunk laden with cash. At the time of the alleged offence he "just happened" to be passing Bombay racecourse. On the spur of the moment he ordered his driver to stop, subtracted "several handfuls" of 100-rupee banknotes from the trunk, entered the racecourse and put the lot on the favourite in the next race.

To prove larceny, he told me, the prosecution would first have to prove larcenous intent. There was no such intent, he said, as had every intention of repaying the money after the horse had won. The fact that it had lost was no fault of his. Blame the jockey, he said, but certainly not him. This was an interesting insight into the working of the criminal mind.

I never knew what happened to him. By the time his trial came up I was well on my way home and perhaps already there. I think that inevitably he would have been tried, found guilty and cashiered. Cashiering is a punishment, severer than dismissal which, according to Chamber's Dictionary, is imposed only on army or naval officers. (No mention is made of RAF officers.) On release, as an ex-Army captain, my guardee could easily have found a job without the necessity of revealing that he was an ex-prisoner. Perhaps his family, nor his friends, nor anybody would never know of his past.

Had his crime been committed in an earlier century matters would have been very different. Cashiering then usually involved a procedure of ritualised

Humiliation. The accused was paraded in front of the entire regiment. The charge and sentence were read out and then, to a prolonged roll of the drums, his officer's badges of rank would have been torn from his uniform by the commanding officer and cast to the ground. He would thus have been formally reduced to the ranks and marched away to a period of close confinement and then to the dreaded Army glasshouse. Here he would suffer periods of physical abuse, pack drill and a bread and water diet.

O.C.T.U.

The course at Llandrindrod Wells was for three months, based on the regime at Sandhurst. The pupils were, like me, 'cadets'. We were to be turned into army officers; in particular, light anti-aircraft gunners trained on Bofors guns which had superseded Lewis guns. I had fired them many times myself with an acceptable level of success at firing camps etc. I would now have to learn how to teach other men to use them. Old Clever Dick here thought he already knew everything there was to be known about Bofors guns after all his time using them at Scunthorpe, North Coates etc. I was reckoning without Gunner Murgatroyd, one of our most untalented gunners who was from Bootle and almost totally illiterate and innumerate. He could count to six but totally incapable of visualising what seven of anything looked like. On one occasion, he was on 'Stag' duty on one of my gun sites. 'Stag' is an Army word for 'Guard' or 'Lookout'. Duty of a gun site stag was to see that nobody stole the gun (possible only if this were a Lewis gun) and keep a sharp look-out for the enemy, especially if in the form of enemy aircraft. This is why we all had to be very good at Aircraft Recognition. Suddenly without any warning our Divisional Commander, a Brigadier, hove into view bent on a snap inspection. This we considered an underhand ploy as it left no time for us to clear up any half-drunk mugs of tea or other detritus. The desired element of surprise was totally negated by the red band round his cap which befitted his rank, and was clearly identified by us with binoculars from half a mile away. With horror, I suddenly noticed that the 'Stag' man was none other than our Gunner Murgatroyd. As the Brigadier approached him an aircraft few directly overhead. We all knew from its distinctive noise that it was a twin-engine Beau fighter from nearby North Coates, possibly on a harmless practice run. "Now then, Gunner", said the Brig, "what sort of plane is that?" Gunner Murgatroyd shielded his eyes with a hand and after a long pause, eventually said, proudly and confidently, "It's a Heinkel VIII", (a German bomber).

"Then why", said the Brig, "the hell are you not shooting at it?" Gunner Murgatroyd looked at our Lewis gun and then the Brig and said "Don't know how to use it, Sir". At Llandrindrod Wells we were lodged at an enormous barrack of a Victorian hotel, The Gwalior. The bedrooms were equipped with black iron bedsteads of the school dormitory type. The Army quickly threw these out as they took up too much room and substituted straw palliaases, 16 to each bedroom. This was early in May 1941. On May 12, in the early morning, while folding up our palliaases for the day, we were astonished to hear on the radio an interruption to 'Housewives Choice' the sensational news that Rudolph Hess, the Fuehrer's right hand man had flown the 800 miles from Augsbury, Germany to Scotland, piloting himself in a Messerschmidt 110 and baled out near Glasgow and offered a cup of coffee by a home guard. The news item said that he was here on a peace mission, convinced the Germans had won the war and was now giving us the chance to exit without further loss to ourselves. This news was no good at all to me as I had no intention of finishing with the Army until I had my commission. It soon transpired that Hess would be locked up in the Tower and would be tried for war crimes at the Nuremberg war crimes tribunal for his trouble and that would be the end of the matter. There would certainly be no end of war or truce.

Statistics showed that 95% of the cadets passed the O.C.T.U. course and were awarded commissions. The Army was anxious to pass as many as possible as it was desperately short of trained artillery officers. However, failure, rare though it was, could come at any moment without warning or reason.

There was no appeal. No second chance. Once out, you were out. For ever. Fear of failure was the one spur that drove us on. There was one cadet on my section that had no such fear. He was tall, good looking, well-spoken, athletic and in classes always first with the right answer. He, I thought, could not possibly fail. But, half way through the course, after a first parade of the day, he was handed his interim report form and told to take it to the adjutant. He did so and was shown that it was endorsed with the feared inscription 'R.T.U.' This meant 'Return to Unit'. Life for him, as a cadet officer, was finished. He protested and asked for a reason so that he may avoid any mistakes he may have made in the future. He was then shown an addendum to his report which said 'L.M.F.' Everybody in the O.C.T.U. would know that his means 'Lacks Moral Fibre', i.e. gutless and not officer material. This hurtful and possibly inaccurate assessment would finish most of us for life. I never saw or heard of him again.

At the end of the course there was a splendid celebratory dinner dance at one of the big hotels. It was said that some of the town girls had engaged each other in fisticuffs to get a ticket. Then, after a short leave, we were off to the Royal Artillery Depot, Woolwich. This famous establishment was luxurious in the extreme with separate bedrooms for each officer, (and there were several hundred of us) and a Mess famous for the quality of its food and its large stock of delicious 1890 very old Madeira wine, which had been sitting in its cellars since the end of the Peninsula War. We were told that we were to get rid of as much of the drink as possible before the bombs got it. It was ten old pence a schooner and we did our best to oblige. A small charge was made as a Mess fee to supplement Army rations, about two pounds a week and well worth it.

There was a theatre there, of the music-hall type and first class shows were staged almost every night. Admission was entirely free. Leading artists appeared, usually without charge as it was such a prestigious slot for them with BBC live coverage. We were all on standby for foreign postings and had to be ready at short notice. We spent almost every day in London. We knew we were bound for the Far East or, if was still there, Singapore. Each of us was given thirty pounds for the purchase of tropical kit and advised that it was obtainable at Allkit in Cambridge Circus. This we did and were quick to realise, on arrival in Bombay, that it was hideously old-fashioned, badly cut and unusable, even as funeral shrouds. Mine was immediately thrown away, every piece of it.

At the Transit Camp we were quickly surrounded by a crowd of Touts wanting to escort us around a nearby bazaar, and in particular, obviously, to their master's shop. One of them was a lad of not more than ten. He was clean and tidy, polite and spoke excellent English.

"You pay be nothing, Sahib! You just look! Just look, costs nothing! I do the buying and save you much money!" I pointed to my unwearable Allkit Service Tunic and khaki drill trousers. "These are very bad, Sahib, not pukka", said my lad. He took me to a store which was not a shop in the general sense but tables piled high with bush jackets and khaki trousers. There were a few Singer sewing machines with operators ready to take instant alterations. I said it was just what I was looking for as I had notices that all officers I had already seen at the camp were wearing similar garments. My lad button-holed the proprietor. "This sahib", he said to the proprietor, "is very big important man and he not want any your fancy prices. You do him good deal and he send many of his friends". I was delighted with my kit, which survived many sessions of thrashings on rocks by dhobis (clothes washers) in rivers. They lasted me the whole time I was in India.

I have already described the difference between shock and fright. I am not going into all that again. I tasted both emotions twice, together, during the War. On the first occasion I was walking along a jungle path in single file of about ten men. I was not at the head, or rear, but in the middle which would have been usual. Visibility was intermittent, because of the thick coppice of bamboo and occasionally, only about a yard. Suddenly there was a loud crashing noise of some huge object crashing its way through the jungle. As it saw our men, it slammed its brakes on, passed and I saw it was a monstrously large Burmese black buck, a stag-like creature without horns about its head, which was half a ton of weight, the size of a large pony, a mouth flecked with foam and it stood there shivering with fright, or shock and pausing just long enough to wonder whether to charge through us or jump over us. On the jump and in the process he cropped my head with a hoof and chipped off my Frank Sinatra fibreglass hat. It galloped off into the jungle and, amazingly, I was unhurt. But shocked? Yes.

My second dice with death was on the final night of my time in India. I had decided to have dinner, alone, at the Cricket Club, where there was a fine dining room overlooking the floodlit play fields ringed with palm trees. Having finished my dinner, and given the waiter an extra generous tip, I left by the front door and turned right for the moonlit stroll back to the transit camp. Simultaneously some 'badnashe' terrorists had removed the club's piano from the dining room, up ended it then carried it to the lift and then to the flat roof. Club employees watched them do this but assessed they were legitimate workmen.

Once on the roof they balanced the piano on the front parapet. Then all they had to do was wait for a suitable target walking on the pavement below, (i.e. any Allied Forces Officer, or perhaps me) then, carefully judging the right moment, give the piano a final shove and it fell to the pavement with a loud crash of splintering wood, snapping and twanging piano strings. It had missed me, and my certain death, by no more than a foot.

EPILOGUE

The Boudoir Boys:
<u>Ken Taylor</u> qualified as a dentist after demob. Disdained N.H.S. and created large, successful private practice catering chiefly for wealthy Manchester businessmen.

<u>Peter Rowlands</u> joined Bank of England and married an American girl (one child)

<u>Peter Ridout</u> married a V.A.D. (wartime nurse) and became Town Clerk for Amersham. Died 2003.

<u>Neil Heap:</u> hugely successful post-war career as shipping agent in New York City. Worked and resided in Madison Avenue for 40 years. Did not marry. Died 1997.

<u>The Author</u>: Still with us (if not it).

<u>Orde Wingate</u>: Killed in air crash in last days of war.

<u>John Taylor</u> built up Five Roses Tea into the largest business complex in South Africa. Died suddenly in Durban, 2000.